YOUR KID'S FAVORITE MEALS
MADE HEALTHY!

by: Ashley Buescher

Your Kid's Favorite Meals Made Healthy!
Copyright © 2012 by O'More College of Design
ISBN-10: 0-9860150-2-4
ISBN-13: 978-0-9860150-2-1

Written by Ashley Buescher
Cover design and interior layout by Brianna Miele
All rights reserved. No part of this publication may be reproduced or transmitted in any form or by any means without written permission of the author.

Published by:
O'More Publishing
A Division of O'More College of Design
423 South Margin St.
Franklin, TN 37064 U.S.A.

YOUR KID'S FAVORITE MEALS
MADE HEALTHY!

by: Ashley Buescher

O'MORE
PUBLISHING

CONTENTS

Introduction ... 1
The Basics to Eating Healthy ... 3
Tips For You ... 12

1

BEVERAGES ... 21

Cranberry Cocktail ... 23
Creamsicle Crush ... 23
Smoothies ... 23
Summer Slush ... 23
Vanilla "Milkshake" ... 25

2

BREADS & BREAKFAST ... 27

Sugar Conversion Chart ... 29
Apple Pie Breakfast ... 31
Nana's Banana Bread ... 31
Biscuits ... 33
Breakfast Casserole ... 33
Breakfast Pizza ... 35
Breakfast Sandwich ... 35
Cinnamon Rolls ... 37
Nana's Cranberry Orange Bread ... 39
Crepes ... 41
Frittata ... 41
Garlic Parmesan Toast ... 43
Granola Parfait ... 43
Muffins ... 43
Reese's Toast ... 47

Nutella ... 47
Powdered Sugar ... 47
Scones ... 49
Whole Wheat Pastries ... 49
Pop Tarts ... 51
Turnovers ... 51
Nana's Zucchini Bread ... 53

SOUPS ... 55

Butternut Squash and Green Apple ... 57
Carrot ... 57
Chicken Noodle ... 59
Chili ... 59
Corn Chowder ... 61
Potato ... 63
Tortilla ... 63
Vegetable ... 65

MEALS ... 67

Annie's Chicken Tenders... 73
Baked Herbed Cheese and Chicken Roll Ups ... 73
Cabbage and Sausage ... 75
Miss Dottie's Chicken Casserole ... 75
Chicken Enchiladas ... 77
Chicken Parmesan ... 77
Chicken Spaghetti (Version 1) ... 79
Chicken Spaghetti (Version 2) ... 81
Daddy's Asian Beef and Rice ... 83
Daddy's Marinara ... 85
Fettuccine Alfredo ... 85
Grilled Cauliflower ... 87

Island Chicken ... 87
Lasagna ... 89
Lasagna II ... 89
Mac'n'Cheese ... 89
Manicotti or Stuffed Pasta Shells ... 91
Mashed Potatoes ... 91
Meatloaf ... 93
Mexican Corn ... 95
Mexican Rice ... 95
Mushroom Rice ... 97
Pizza ... 97
Pizza Burgers ... 99
Pork Tenderloin and Sweet Couscous ... 99
Rainbow Rice ... 99
Risotto ... 101
Shells'n'Cheese ... 103
Southwest Chicken ... 103
Sweet and Sour Chicken ... 105
Taco Casserole ... 107
Taco Pockets ... 107

5

SANDWICHES ... 109

Cheesy Ranch Roll-Ups ... 111
Happy Hummus ... 113
Stuffed Peanut Butter Pouch ... 113
Tomato & Mozarella ... 113
Turkey Monte Cristo ... 115

6

SNACKS ... 117

Bugs on a Stick ... 119
Corn Dip ... 119
Cucumber Bites ... 119
Fruit Roll Ups ... 121
Granola Bites ... 121
Mini Pizzas ... 123
Pita Chips ... 123
Rainbow Fruit Skewers ... 125
Salmon Squares ... 125
Veggie Squares ... 125
Shrimp Dip ... 127
Spinach Dip ... 127
Turkey Tails ... 129

7

SWEET TOOTH ... 137

Sugar Conversion Chart ... 139
Banana Split ... 141
Banana Pudding ... 141
Bread Pudding ... 143
Brownies ... 143
Mom's Butter Cookies ... 145
Cheesecake ... 147
Chocolate Cake ... 149
Nana's Cola Cake ... 153
Chocolate Chip Cookies ... 153
Fruit Cobbler ... 155
Granola Balls ... 157
Grape Dessert ... 157
Powdered Sugar ... 157
Strawberry Shortcake ... 159
Yellow Cake ... 161

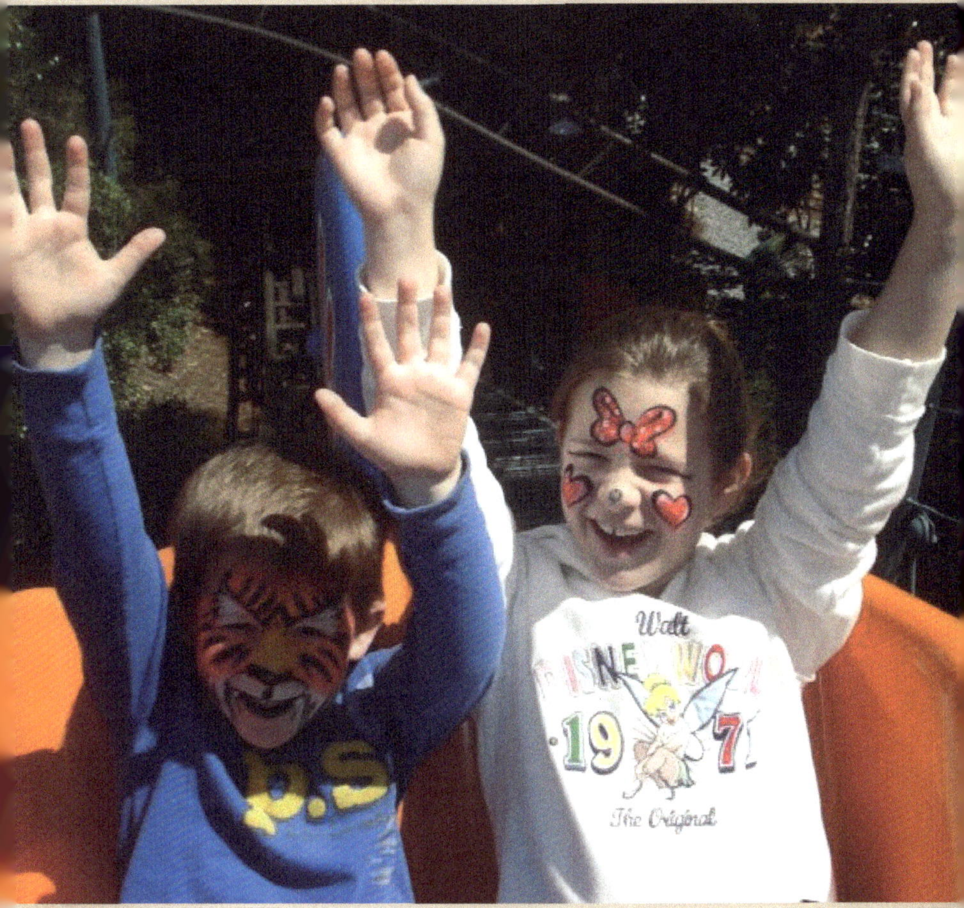
Walt
The Original

INTRODUCTION

My name is Ashley Buescher. If I can transform my family's eating habits into healthy habits, YOU certainly can too!! I am a mother of three girls, ages 14, 10, and infant. In addition, I am a family nurse practitioner, and I work outside the home. Furthermore, I have a sweet tooth the size of a skyscraper which makes eating healthy a challenge. However, I had no choice but to change the eating habits in my household. I made the changes and have written this book for two reasons.

One reason for writing this book is a personal reason. A medical issue directly related to eating habits hit one of my children in January 2012. I had no choice but to change all of our eating habits and change them quickly. To jumpstart this new lifestyle, my husband and I threw away four large trash bags of all food that contained white flour and/or white sugar. FOUR bags! I was not sure if I felt relieved or sickened. In addition, we threw away diet soft drinks. As I stared with pride at my empty cabinets and half empty fridge, I thought, "Ok, now what?" Well, hours and hours of research, trial and error food options, and dealing with children's resistance was what.

Making the lifestyle change in my home was not exactly a smooth process, and I certainly made mistakes. Actually, we still have to work at it on a daily basis. My goal in writing this book is to help your family transition into a healthier lifestyle as seamless as possible. I have taken the majority of the work out of the process for you. In addition, I hope to guide you so that you avoid the mistakes I made. I learned very quickly in our process, that if my children felt deprived, the transition was never going to work. Therefore, I performed a healthy makeover on all of their favorite foods. They did not feel deprived and I did not worry about what they were eating when served in appropriate portions.

Another thing I learned in my family's process was that the transformation was going to go much smoother with peer support. This meant having friends over after school or for dinner and offering healthy snack options or meals. In addition, having friends over who enjoyed being active was helpful. Whether this meant riding bikes or doing 30 minutes of Wii Dance Party, the kids were having fun exercising together. My children felt reassured and good about sharing this lifestyle change with peers. By now we all know that choices children and adults make will be influenced by lifestyles of those around them. Society focuses so much on kids influencing kids in making negative lifestyle choices. I feel society needs to focus on kids influencing one another to make positive lifestyle choices. There is no greater "high" than eating right and exercising!!!

The second reason I wrote this book stems from my profession. As a nurse practitioner, I perform physical exams and health screens on children ages 3-18 in the public school system in Memphis, TN. If you were not already aware, one in three children in the U.S. is overweight or obese. In 2011-2012, out of 52,000 plus children seen, my company referred 30% of those for being overweight or being obese. In addition, a large number of these children were also diagnosed with high blood pressure, high cholesterol, or diabetes. This percentage does not include the children we identified as being at risk for becoming overweight later in life.

Why is the trend of obesity and related disease out of control in our children (and adults)? The trend of obesity is out of control because we do not watch portions, and we do not watch calories. Even worse, we eat too many processed foods. I will discuss this in more detail later, but in short, processed foods are nothing but harmful, empty calories that lead to life threatening diseases. I was very guilty of stocking my household with processed foods as they were convenient for my busy lifestyle. I'm not stocking them anymore.

To read more about obesity in our nation visit www.heart.org

Please note I do not claim to be an expert. I am not a chef. I am not a food artist. I am not a registered dietician. I am a parent with a medical background sharing my experience with you. The photos of food are from my kitchen and surroundings representing my true experience with the recipes. The photos of the children were submitted by parents who are my friends and family.

THE BASICS TO EATING HEALTHY

How do you know if your child is overweight or at risk for being overweight? To determine whether or not your child is overweight or at risk for becoming overweight, you need to know their Body Mass Index or BMI. The BMI is calculated based on an individual's height and weight. The results will tell you if your child is underweight, a healthy weight, at risk for being overweight, or obese. To calculate your child's BMI go to www.bmi-calculator.net

Where do I start? The first thing I knew I had to do was find healthy alternatives for the foods my children enjoyed (that I threw away). We already utilized some of these alternatives, but I felt sharing all of them was important.

Instead of...	Try...	Examples
White flour	Whole wheat flour (not "wheat," but "*whole* wheat")	Whole wheat bread, whole wheat tortillas, whole wheat pancake/waffle mix, whole wheat pizza crust, whole wheat all purpose flour or coconut flour for baking
White rice	Brown rice or quinoa	
Regular pasta	Whole wheat pasta	

Why? White flour goes through a refining process which strips the original form of approximately 80 percent of nutrients that is found in unrefined whole wheat flour. As a result, the body does not recognize white flour as a wheat source which could be utilized slowly as a good source of energy. Instead, the body sees white flour as a pure carbohydrate which means your body sees white flour as pure sugar (discussed below)! If that is not enough, white flour is white due to bleaching which puts you and your children at risk for exposure to harmful chemicals. In addition, white rice and pasta endure the same process of stripping the original form of bran, wheat germ, and other nutrients stripped through processing.

Instead of...	Try...
White sugar	Agave nectar, honey, Stevia, Splenda, xylitol, or erythritol

Why? Where do I begin? Once again, sugar is refined as discussed above and is essentially nothing but added calories in the diet. The consumption of sugar leads to a vicious dietary cycle:

Sugar -> spike in insulin levels -> body stores sugar as fat -> insulin levels crash ->you crash-> hunger craving for carbs ->weight gain

As a result of this dietary cycle, refined sugar is directly linked to multiple health conditions such as obesity, diabetes, cancer, yeast infections, and decreased immunity, just to name a few. In short, refined sugar is *terrible* for you.

For more information visit www.livestrong.com or www.mayoclinic.com

Substitutes for refined sugar: These days, everyone has his or her opinion regarding artificial sweeteners, and we will keep it that way. I will provide information on safe options I discovered, but I want you to use an alternative you are comfortable with. I am simply sharing my experience. For starters, my child's endocrinologist recommended Splenda. According to the studies and articles I have read, I have not seen conclusive evidence that Splenda has been proven to be harmful. However, Splenda has not been on the market long enough to collect enough information that the sweetener is not harmful. When using Splenda for baking purposes, I am not always impressed with the taste. Other alternatives for refined sugar include agave nectar, honey, Stevia, Xylitol, or Erythritol. I primarily use agave nectar and Xylitol; however, I will share more information on all five without getting too scientific.

What is agave nectar? Agave nectar is similar to honey in texture. Agave is naturally occurring in the agave plant found in the Southwestern U.S and Mexico. There seems to be debate over whether or not agave nectar is 100% natural once the product is on store shelves. Regardless, agave is much better for you than refined sugar. Agave is easier on the digestive system, and it does not negatively impact blood sugar and insulin levels. Like honey, agave contains calories, but is sweeter than refined sugar meaning you use less. Agave is good for baking and in everyday life to replace syrup, in coffee, in tea, etc. Agave nectar is one of my favorites!
For more information, visit
www.allaboutagave.com
www.realage.com
www.betterworldcookies.com

Why use honey? As discussed earlier, the refining process of food strips the nutrients. Refined sugar is nothing but calories. Although honey contains more calories than refined sugar, honey also contains nutrients, antioxidant and antimicrobial properties. In addition, honey is sweeter than sugar, and less is needed to achieve the desired taste. Both have an effect on blood sugar; however, honey is absorbed and digested slower as compared to refined sugar which hits the blood stream like a torpedo.

What is Stevia? Stevia is a plant-derived natural sweetener. The product is sold in a powder form and liquid form. Truvia is also a product made from Stevia. The product has almost no calories and has no effect on blood sugar levels. I found debate as to the safety of the product. Overall, the research was positive. Stevia is much sweeter than sugar: especially in the liquid form. In addition, Stevia is best with bold flavors such as coffee, chocolate, sauces, lemon, berries, etc. Stevia is good for baking or for everyday uses.

For more information, visit
www.eatingwell.com
www.stevia.com

What is Xylitol? During my initial research efforts, xylitol was an intimidating word that I would usually skim over. When I stopped being intimidated, I was pleasantly surprised that "this word" is an ideal substitute for refined sugar. Xylitol is a naturally occurring sugar that is extracted from berries and mushrooms. Xylitol comes in a powdered form and is low-calorie and has zero net carbs. However, xylitol is not a product that can be easily found in my local grocery stores. Most Whole Foods carry the product; although, I am unable to find it in mine. Ordering online is a guarantee to finding xylitol. There are several sites, including Amazon, that carry the product.

For more information, visit www.xylitol.org

What is Erythritol? Erythritol is a plant-derived natural sweetener and classified as a sugar alcohol. Sugar alcohols are not utilized as an energy source, but do provide for a good sugar substitute. The product has virtually no calories and does not affect blood sugar levels or insulin levels. Typically, the product is 70% as sweet as refined sugar; although, some companies will claim their product is "as sweet" as refined sugar. I found that erythritol was highly recommended as a substitute and is found in a granulated and powdered form. However, the product is difficult to find on the store shelf. Once again, ordering the product online is your best option.

For more information, visit
www.altmedicine.com
www.zsweet.com
www.yourhealtheducator.com

What about raw sugar? Well, although "raw sugar" sounds healthy, sugar is sugar. Some forms of raw sugar may not be as processed as white sugar, but the health risks are the same.

Do you use Nutella? Prior to my research, I was one of those moms who thought Nutella was a healthy alternative to chocolate. The first and key ingredient is sugar!! Needless to say, I quickly found a "replacement" recipe which you will find in the *"Breads & Breakfast"* section. There are also a few products online.

How do I know how to correctly substitute the above alternatives for refined sugar? The following is a conversion chart for sugar substitutes and refined sugar in regards to baking. I will include this chart again in the *"Breads & Breakfast"* and in the *"Sweet Tooth"* section of the book for easy access.

	Ratio to refined sugar	Comments
Agave Nectar	Multiply amount of sugar x 2/3 = amount of agave	Decrease liquids in recipes by ¼ to 1/3 for every 2/3 cup agave
Erythritol	1:1	May increase amount according to your taste
Honey	Multiply amount of sugar x 2/3 = amount of honey	
Stevia liquid	1 tsp:1 cup sugar	
Stevia powder	1:1	Add 10% liquid in recipes
Splenda granulated	1:1	
Splenda sugar blend	½:1	
Splenda brown sugar blend	½:1 (to substitute for brown sugar)	
Xylitol	1:1	May decrease amount according to your taste as xylitol is sweet

For more information, visit www.replacesugar.com

Instead of...	Try...
Regular peanut butter	Natural peanut butter or PB2 Crunch

Why? Regular peanut butter contains hydrogenated oils. Hydrogenated oils are processed oils added to food to prolong shelf life and add flavor. Some experts refer to hydrogenated oils as "poison." Without getting too scientific, they activate a hormone in the body that is responsible for high blood pressure, blood clotting, heart attack, high LDL (bad cholesterol), low HDL (good cholesterol), and decreases the body's ability to fight against cancer and disease. Natural peanut butter does not contain hydrogenated oils. At least, they should not contain hydrogenated oils. Check the label. PB2 Crunch does not contain hydrogenated oils either.

For more information on the dangers of hydrogenated oils, visit www.becomehealthynow.com

What is PB2 Crunch? PB2 Crunch is a powdered peanut butter I discovered through a friend a few months ago. You add water to the powder, and you get a creamy peanut butter! The nutritional value is unbeatable, and my family doesn't even notice the difference. In addition, the powder blends easily in healthy shakes. PB2 Crunch is one of the best products I discovered on this journey!! Below is a nutritional comparison chart:

2 Tbsp	Fat	Calories	Protein	Hydrogenated Oils
Regular Peanut Butter	16	190	8	Yes
Natural Peanut Butter	16	190	8	No
PB2 Crunch	1	45	5	No

To order PB2 Crunch, visit www.netrition.com

Instead of...	Try...
Ground beef	Ground breast of turkey, fish, chicken, or tofu

Why? Simply put, ground breast of turkey, chicken, fish and tofu all have less fat and calories than ground beef. I think by now, we all understand that less fat and calories leads to better health. Beware, a few years ago while comparing labels, I realized that the nutritional values of ground turkey were not that different from ground beef. Make sure you buy ground breast of turkey. Below is a comparison chart so you may see the differences in nutritional value.

4 oz.	Calories	Fat	Protein	Carbs
85% lean ground beef	272	16g	29g	0g
Ground turkey	193	11g	22g	0g
Ground breast of turkey	130	1.5g	27g	0g
Tuna	120	0g	28g	0g
Tofu (lite)	40	0g	8g	0g

For more information visit www.nutritiondata.self.com

I must be honest regarding tofu. No one in my family will touch tofu; however, tofu is a very healthy choice. In addition, black bean and veggie burgers are healthy alternatives to burgers.

Instead of...	Try...
Fried foods	Baked or grilled foods

Why? To eliminate dangerous fats, calories, and cholesterol.

Instead of...	Try...
Whole eggs	Egg whites or egg beaters

Why? This modification is recommended mainly if you are looking to cut calories and fat. If I am making an omelet, I will use one whole egg and one or two egg whites. The kids see the eggs as the same color due to the yolk while I am cutting their fat and calories. I use egg whites as much as possible; although, throwing away perfectly good yolks can be painful.

Instead of...	Try...
Soft drinks--regular or diet	Water, Crystal Light, or zero calorie flavored water
Juices	Low sugar, low calorie, or sugar free juices (or the above suggestions)

Why? To eliminate sugars, fat, calories, and caffeine which all lead to obesity. Be sure to check labels on flavored waters. I was surprised to find that many contain a good amount of calories. Below is a table for daily water recommendations for children:

Age group in years	Daily Recommendation for Water Intake (1 cup=8oz)
1-3	4 cups

4-8	5 cups
Girls 9-13	7 cups
Boys 9-13	8 cups
Girls 14-18	8 cups
Boys 14-18	11 cups

For more information visit www.kraftrecipes.com

Instead of...	Try...
Whole milk or 2% milk	Skim milk

Why? To eliminate fat and calories.

Instead of...	Try...
Ice cream	Fat free, sugar free sorbet, sherbet, or frozen fat free whipped topping

Why? To eliminate fat and calories.

11

TIPS FOR YOU

One mistake I was making prior to my child's diagnosis was neglecting correct portion sizes. As a result, my children were eating larger portions than they were supposed to; therefore, they were eating more calories. I guess this one mistake actually counts as two mistakes.

In order to help you avoid these mistakes, I have included two charts below. The first chart represents daily recommended portions for children. The second represents daily calorie recommendations for children.

	Servings/day	1-3yrs (1 serving =)	4-5yrs (1 serving =)	6-12yrs (1 serving =)	12-Adult (1 serving =)
Vegetables	3-5	¼ cup	1/3 cup	½ cup	½ cup
Fruits	2-4	¼ cup	1/3 cup	½ cup	½ cup
Pasta, Grains, Breads, Cereals	5 or less	½ slice or ¼ cup	½ slice or 1/3 cup	1 slice or ½ cup	1 slice or ½ cup
Milk/Milk Products	2-3	½ cup	¾ cup	1 cup	1 cup
Meat/Protein	2-3	1oz or ¼ cup	1.5oz or ¾ cup	2oz or ½ cup	2-3oz or ½ cup

For more information visit www.permanente.net

This is what your plate should look like! Coming soon to www.kickinitkids.com

Age	1yr	2-3yrs	4-8yrs	9-13yrs	14-18yrs
Daily Calories	900	1000			
Daily Calories for Females			1200	1600	1800
Daily Calories for Males			1400	1800	2200

For more information visit www.livestrong.com

Reading food labels is also important to help avoid incorrect portions and calories.

What am I looking for when reading a food label? I have been reading labels for as long as I can remember. Nutrition food labels can be difficult to understand. I wanted to share some tips when reading food labels.

- Read the ingredients list! Typically, the first ingredient is the primary ingredient used to make the food item. If that first ingredient is sugar, white flour, or a word you cannot pronounce, you might want to leave the item on the shelf.
- Read the portion size. The quickest way to overeat is to eat incorrect portions.
- Beware of sugar free items. Just because an item is sugar free, does not mean the item is low in calories or carbs. It is important to look at those values also.
- Beware of fat-free items. Often fat-free products are loaded with sugar to maintain flavor.
- Read more into "percentages." If a product says "95% fat free," how much fat did the product have before? Check the fat value beyond the large font label percentage.
- Read past "lower" or "reduced." Once again, lower or reduced as compared to what before? For example, a

13

product can be "lower in sodium" and still contain a large amount of sodium.

Below is a chart representing daily recommendations for nutritional values seen on food labels. Keep in mind, these daily recommendations fluctuate slightly depending on who is making the recommendation.

Age	2-3yrs	4-8yrs	9-13yrs	14-18yrs
Fat	33g-54g	39g-62g	62g-85g	Girls: 55g-78g Boys: 61g-95g
Saturated Fat	12g-16g	16g-18g	Girls: 18g-22g Boys: 20g-24g	Girls: 22g Boys: 24g-27g
Carbohydrates	113g-116g	135g-195g	Girls: 158g-228g Boys: 180g-260g	Girls: 203g-293g Boys: 225g-325g
Protein	13g	19g	34g	Girls: 46g Boys: 52g
Sodium	1000mg-1500mg	1200mg-1900mg	1500mg-2200mg	1500mg-2300mg
Cholesterol	<300mg	<300mg	<300mg	<300mg
Fiber	14g-19g	19g-23g	Girls: 23g-28g Boys: 25g-31g	31g-34g

For more information, visit
www.livestrong.com
www.mayoclinic.com
www.bcm.edu

What is the difference between saturated and unsaturated fats? You will see fat broken down into types on a food label. Below is a chart to sum up the differences:

Types of Fats	Saturated Fats	Unsaturated Fats
Source	Derived from animal products	Derived from fruits and vegetables

Health Effects	Increases LDL (bad) cholesterol & decreases HDL (good) cholesterol. Consumption may lead to heart disease & artherosclerosis	Decreases LDL(bad) cholesterol & increases HDL (good) cholesterol
Foods	Butter, margarine, whole milk, peanut butter, coconut oil, cheese, vegetable oil, fish oil	Olive oil, canola oil, soybean oil, sesame oil, corn oil avocado, olives, nuts

For more information visit
www.mayoclinic.com
www.lowfatcooking.about.com
www.diffen.com

What is the difference between simple carbohydrates and complex carbohydrates? Carbohydrates are broken down into two classes according to the chemical structure and on how quickly the body digests and absorbs the carbohydrate. Below is a chart to sum up the differences:

	Simple Carbohydrate	Complex Carbohydrate
Chemical Structure	Comprised of 1 or 2 sugars	Comprised of 3 or more sugars
Absorption/Digestion	Quickly	Slowly
Health Effects	-Very few nutrients -Mainly empty calories -Stored as fat if not utilized -Attributes to obesity	-Contain Fiber -Utilized by body as source of energy
Food Examples	Good: Fruit and Milk Bad: candy, soft drinks, jelly	Green vegetables, corn, legumes, potatoes, bread, rice, and pasta

For more information visit
www.diabetes.about.com
www.nutritionmd.org

My biggest challenge for portion control was with snacks.

What is the best way to control snack choices and portions? First of all, I quickly replaced all the food I threw out with healthier food choices. Now what? It just so happens I was reading the book *PUSH* by Chalene Johnson. She provided excellent advice regarding snacking:

- Fill Ziploc snack bags and small Gladware/Tupperware containers with healthy snacks with exact portions according to food labels.
- Place all snacks where they are eye level for the kids. For example, take all fruit and vegetable snack bags out of the produce drawers and onto an eye level shelf. Do the same for the pantry.
- Snack suggestions: whole wheat pretzel sticks, lightly salted peanuts mixed with unsalted peanuts, 100 calories popcorn bags, grapes, melon, strawberries, carrots, and hardboiled egg whites.
- I also placed low-fat string cheese, turkey pinwheels, and hummus on the eye level refrigerator shelf.
- As far as the pantry, I organized the snacks in shallow bins so the snacks would not be shoved behind something else.

The last mistake I am about to tell you about is the one that sparked my venture for writing this book. I made too many drastic changes too fast. We completely went "cold turkey" with the food changes, and that was a bad idea. My children felt deprived, and that led to a lot of resistance. Below are some actions that proved effective.

- Find healthy alternatives to their favorite dinners and introduce 2-3 a week. By finding these alternatives, my children did not feel deprived, and there was no resistance when the vegetable/protein/starch meals were served.
- Engage your child in meal preparation. Cooking with your children provides for great quality time with your children, plus they are more excited to eat their "masterpiece." In addition, they will encourage others to try it.

17

- Do not isolate your child from treats at birthday parties, school parties, etc. If they have treats on special occasions, just balance the rest of the day out.
- My middle child enjoys diet sodas. I no longer keep them in the house, but she is free to enjoy one if we go out to dinner or to a function of some sort. No refills. Once again, she does not feel deprived, and she is losing her interest in diet sodas.
- Buying lunch at school was something we had to cut out. After our initial three month boycott, I started letting her circle 2-3 days/month on the lunch calendar on which she wanted to buy lunch. I did not make one comment on her choices. I would just adjust the rest of the day accordingly. Again, she did not feel deprived and actually changed her mind on the circled days most of the time.
- The "cold turkey" approach to replacing all white flour to whole wheat flour was one I was strict about. Despite resistance initially, my children adapted to the taste within two weeks.
- Also, the "cold turkey" approach to processed snacks was one I was adamant about. Again, their tastes adjusted, and the change was a nonissue within a couple of weeks. Yes, they will have processed snacks here and there, but I do not stock them in my house like I used to.
- Set short term goals when making a lifestyle change. I would recommend setting goals for one week to one month at a time that build towards long term goals. Short term goals are easier to meet which leads to a sense of accomplishment and enthusiasm regarding reaching more goals.
- Most importantly, emphasize to your children the lifestyle change is about becoming HEALTHY and not about losing weight. This actually might be the case for your child, but I am speaking to the parents whose children have weight as an issue.

The second half of this book contains recipes for healthy alternatives to my children's favorite foods. There are hundreds of healthy recipes out there. These recipes pertain to the ones my family made changes with. Hopefully the endless hours of research I spent finding comparable, healthy meals will make eating healthy easier for your family. Plus you now have the tools to recreate any meal.

I left the nutritional values off the recipes on purpose. I wanted to relieve you of the chore of checking calories, fat, and carbohydrates. If you are choosing the right food from the start and controlling portion sizes, you should not have to worry so much about counting calories for every bite of food. From my observations over the years, people will not think twice about eating a burger and fries, but will pick apart labels when trying to "diet." In turn, eating the bad food becomes a pleasurable, carefree experience, and eating right becomes a burden. The goal of this book is that you maintain portion control and maintain healthy alternatives to processed foods. If you follow those suggestions, you should not have to worry about the rest. Eating healthy should be the pleasurable, carefree experience!

As my sugar-addicted, very picky teenage daughter would say: "If I say mom's new recipe is good, then you know it is good!"

BEVERAGES

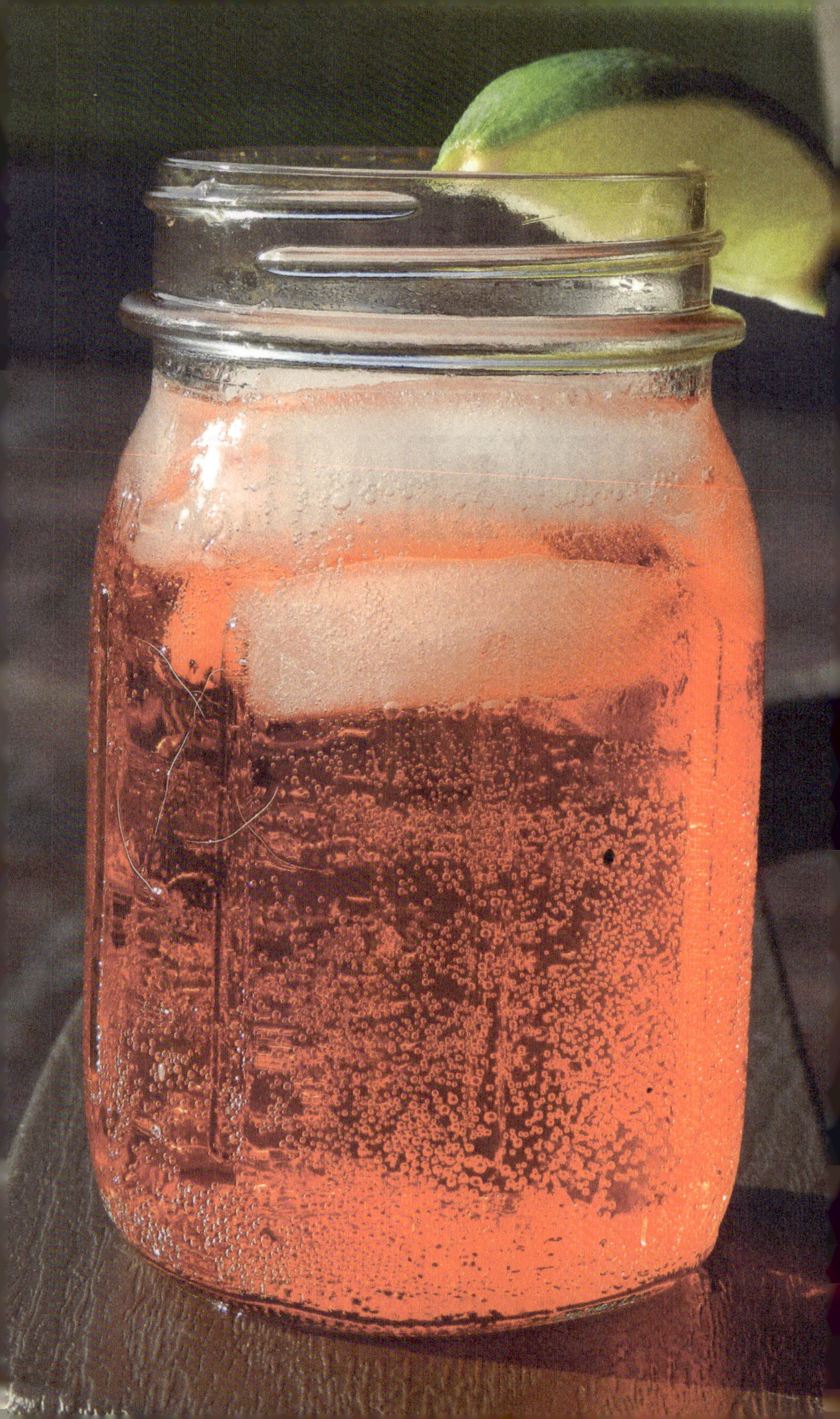

CRANBERRY COCKTAIL

4oz diet cranberry juice
4oz lemon lime sparkling water
1 lime wedge (optional)
Cherries (optional)

- Pour diet cranberry juice and lemon lime seltzer water over ice.
- Add juice from fresh lime wedge if desire.
- Garnish with a lime wedge.

CREAMSICLE CRUSH

1/2 cup of your favorite fat-free, sugar-free sorbet OR sherbet
4oz skim milk (or Crystal Light)
½ cup of favorite fresh fruit (optional)

Blend together or just stir with a spoon.

SMOOTHIES

6oz lowfat or nonfat Greek yogurt
1 cup skim milk
½ to 1 cup of your favorite fruit or berry (do not exceed 1 cup fruit)

Blend and enjoy!

SUMMER SLUSH

8oz of your favorite Crystal Light drink
6 ice cubes (may make ice cubes out of the above flavor of Crystal Light or a complimenting flavor of Crystal light)

Blend Crystal Light drink with 6 regular or 6 flavored ice cubes in a blender and enjoy!

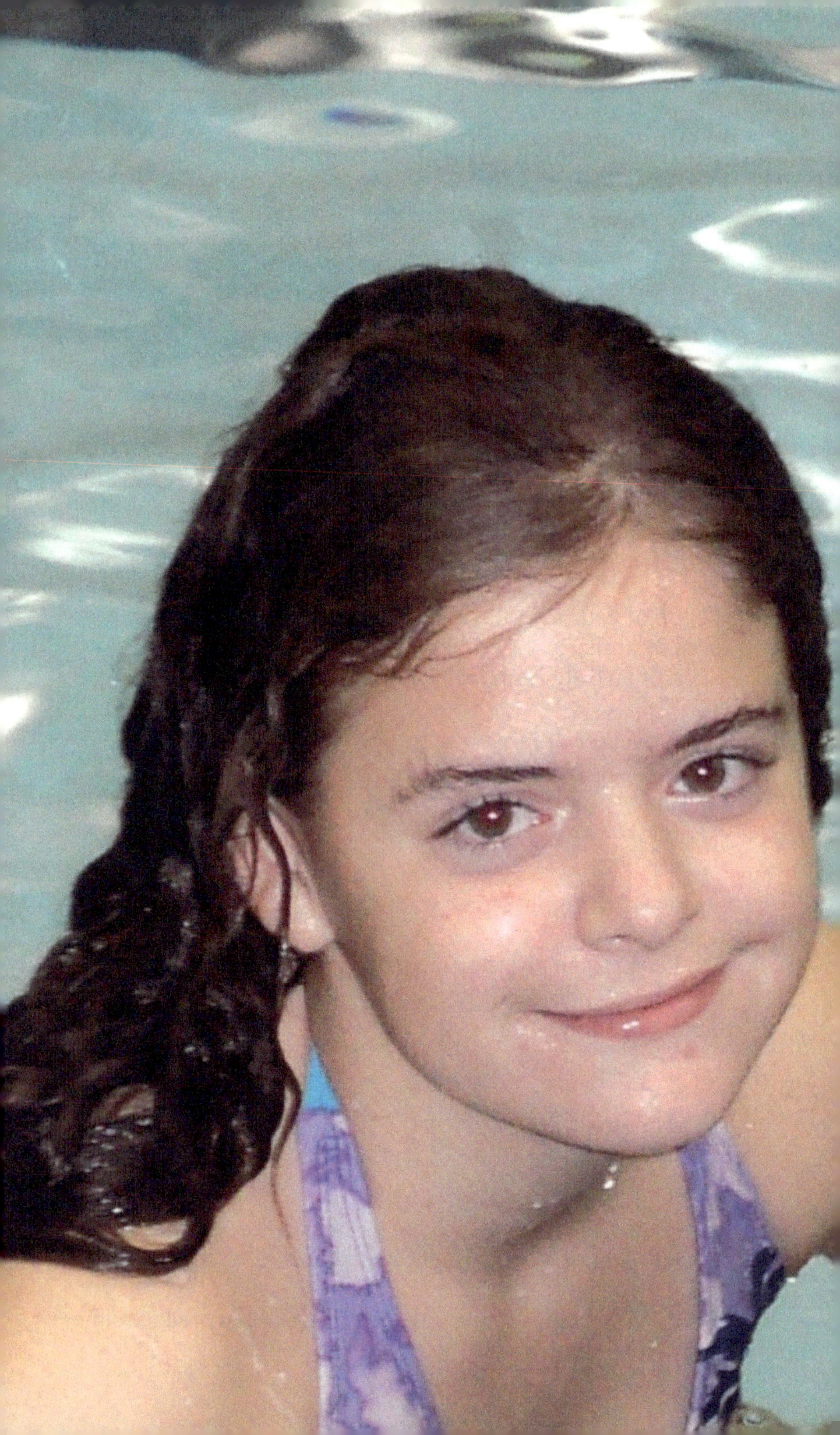

VANILLA "MILKSHAKE"

8oz fat-free milk
1-2 TBSP Sugar Free French Vanilla Coffeemate
1 packet Splenda or tsp liquid sugar substitute (optional)

Mix all together, and it tastes just like a vanilla milkshake!!

BREADS & BREAKFAST

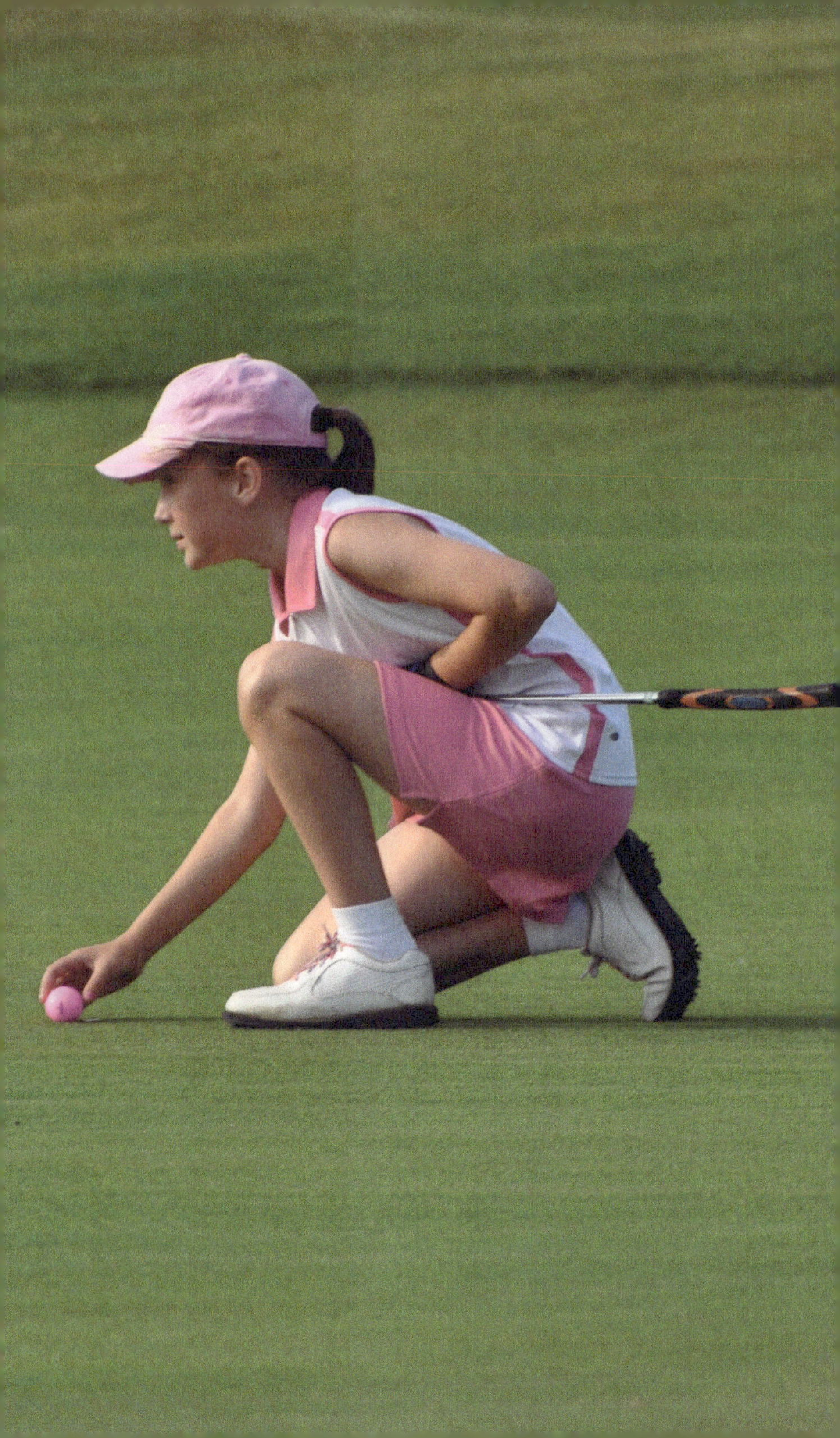

CONVERSION CHART FOR SUGAR SUBSTITUTES

	Ratio to refined sugar	Comments
Agave Nectar	Multiply amount of sugar x 2/3 = amount of agave	Decrease liquids in recipes by ¼ to 1/3 for every 2/3 cup agave
Erythritol	1:1	May increase amount according to your taste
Honey	Multiply amount of sugar x 2/3 = amount of honey	
Stevia liquid	1 tsp:1 cup sugar	
Stevia powder	1:1	Add 10% liquid in recipes
Splenda granulated	1:1	
Splenda sugar blend	½:1	
Splenda brown sugar blend	½:1 (to substitute for brown sugar)	
Xylitol	1:1	May decrease amount according to your taste as xylitol is sweet

I primarily use agave nectar and Xylitol.

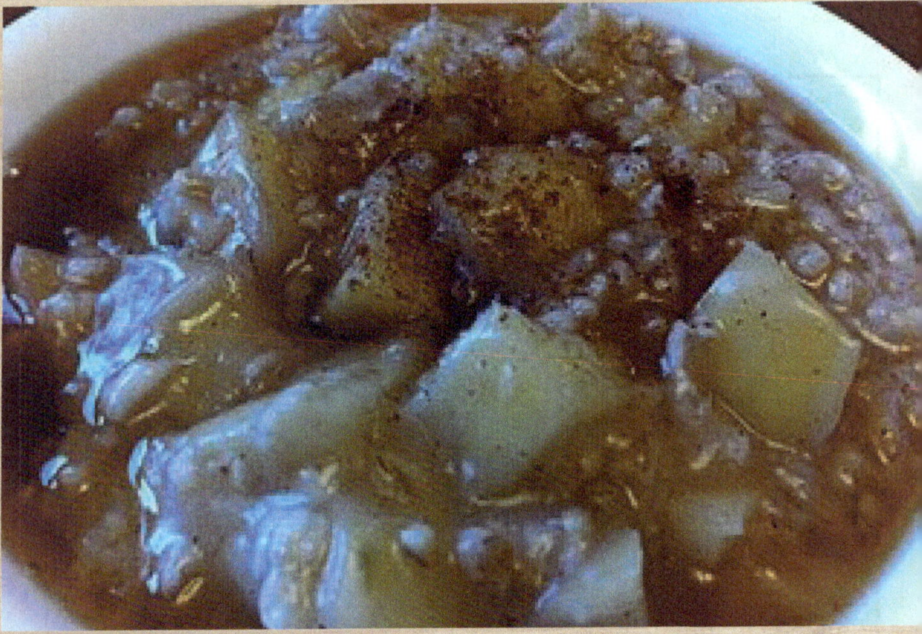

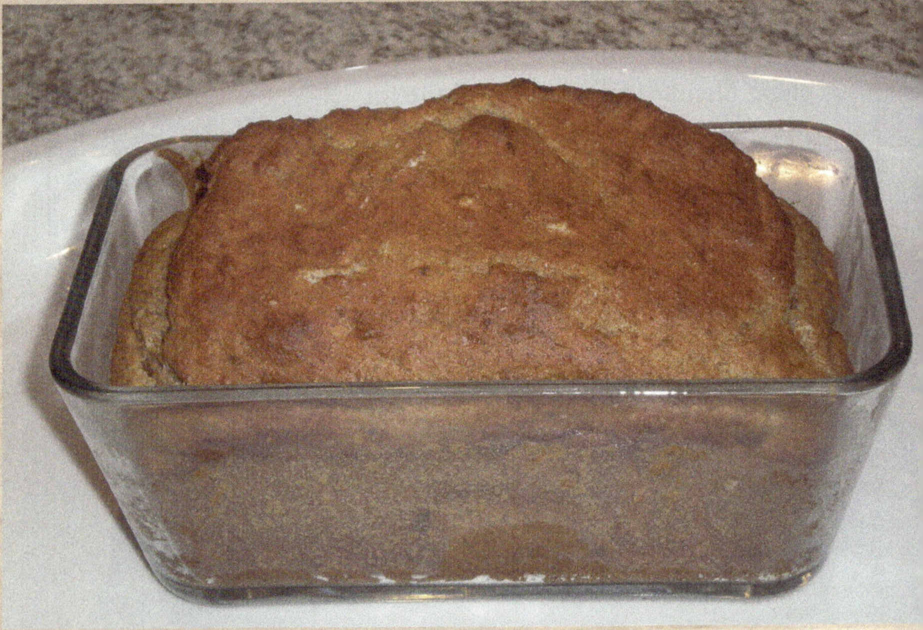

APPLE PIE BREAKFAST
Recipe from "Get Fit With Nicole"

1 cup steel cut oats
3 diced apples
1 cup diet apple juice or regular apple juice
3 cups water
½ tsp cinnamon

Place all ingredients in a crockpot. Cook on low overnight.

NANA'S BANANA BREAD
One serving: 1/12 of loaf

¼ cups whole wheat flour (may use ½ whole wheat, ½ white for longevity)
Sugar substitute for 1 cup sugar (refer to conversion chart)
3 ripe medium bananas
¾ cups skim milk
3 TBSP vegetable oil (coconut or canola)
1 egg or 2 egg whites
3.5 tsp Baking powder (omit if using self-rising flour)
1 tsp Salt (omit if using self-rising flour)

- Preheat oven to 350.
- Mix all ingredients in a mixer on medium speed for 30 seconds scraping sides constantly. *Bread will be "rubbery" if you mix much longer.
- Pour into 9x3x5 greased and floured loaf pan.
- Bake 50 minutes or until toothpick comes out "clean" in center.

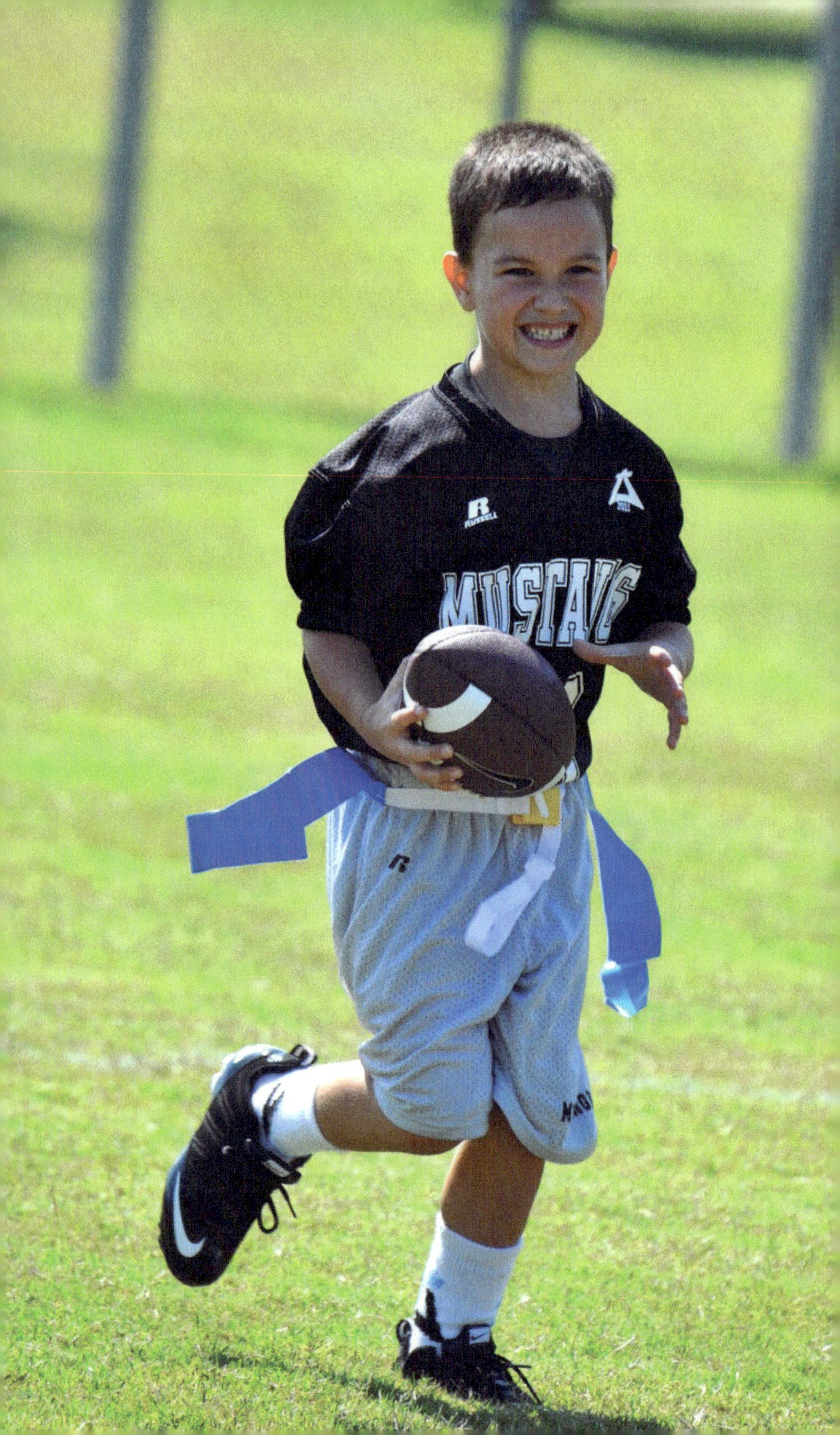

BISCUITS
Adapted from Heart and Soul cookbook

2 cups whole wheat flour
2 cups white all-purpose flour (may use 4 cups whole wheat flour)
1 tsp baking powder
½ tsp baking soda
1 tsp salt
1 cup unsalted softened
2 cups skim milk

- Put first 4 ingredients in mixing bowl and blend.
- Add butter chunks until resembles large crumbs.
- Make a well in center of dough and pour in milk.
- Mix just until the dough sticks together.
- Roll out to ½ inch thickness on floured surface and cut into 2" circles.
- Place on ungreased baking sheet and prick biscuits with a fork.
- Bake 400 for 8-10 minutes.

NOTE: for crisp sided biscuits, place one inch apart. For soft sided, place close together.

BREAKFAST CASSEROLE

8 egg whites and 4 whole eggs OR 2 cups Egg Beaters
1 cups low fat shredded cheddar
1 cup skim milk
4 pack Morning Star sausage patties OR ½ lb turkey sausage
1-2 cups veggies of your choice (optional)
6 slices whole wheat bread (optional)

- Cook sausage according to directions or brown turkey sausage.

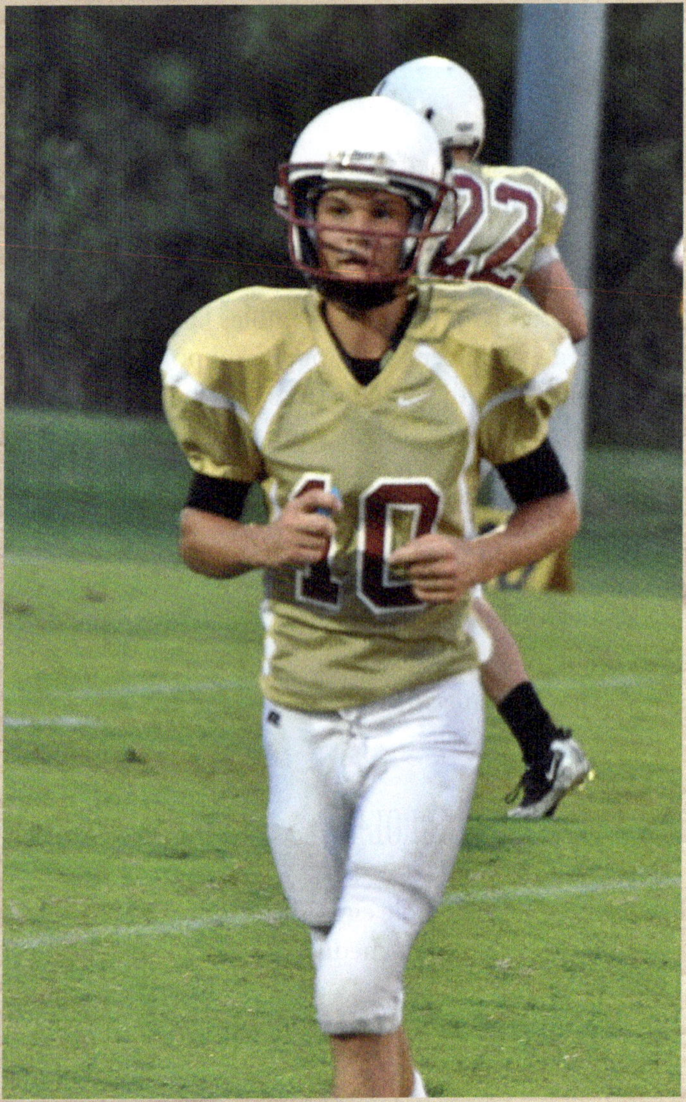
22
10

- Chop and sauté vegetables, if using.
- Mix eggs, cheese, and milk together.
- Salt and pepper egg mixture to taste.
- Coat 9x13 casserole dish with nonstick cooking spray.
- If using bread, cube and spread in bottom of dish.
- If using veggies, spread evenly on top of bread.
- Pour egg mixture over bread and veggies.
- Bake uncovered 350 for 30-40 min.

BREAKFAST PIZZA

1 whole wheat English muffin split
1 whole egg or 2 egg whites
1 TBSP skim milk
2 TBSP salsa
2 TBSP low fat shredded cheese
2 slices turkey pepperoni – optional

- In a small bowl, beat egg and milk with a fork. Scramble or cook in a solid piece over medium heat in small skillet until done.
- Spread a TBSP salsa over each half of the English muffin.
- Place half of cooked egg on top of salsa on each half of English muffin.
- Top each half with 1 TBSP low fat shredded cheese and 1 pepperoni (optional).

BREAKFAST SANDWICH

1 whole wheat English muffin or whole wheat bagel thin
2 egg whites scrambled
1 piece turkey bacon or 1 Morning Star sausage patty or 1 turkey sausage patty
1 TBSP low fat shredded cheddar

Layer egg, meat, and cheese on English muffin or bagel.

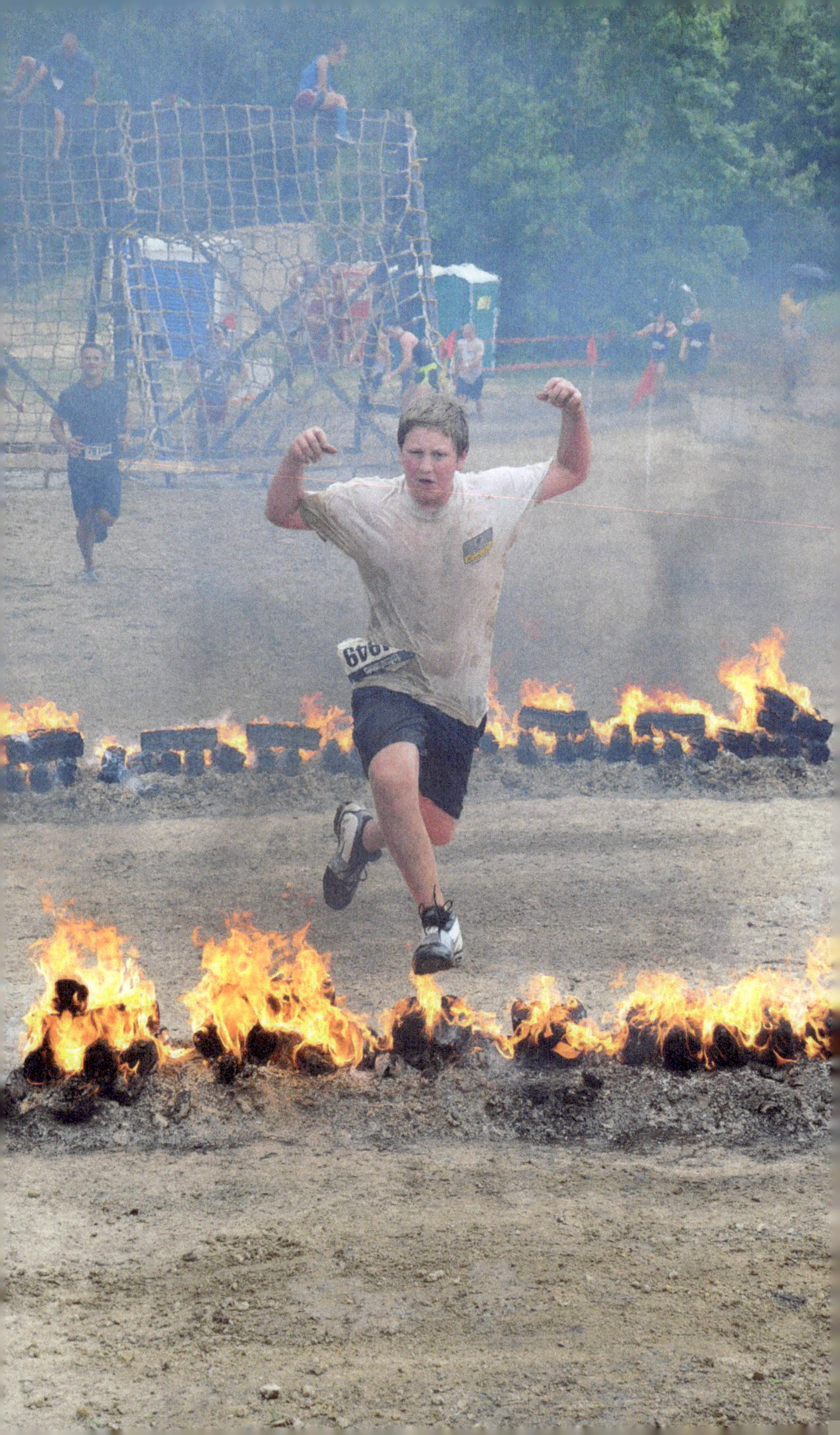

CINNAMON ROLLS
(Grandmama's)

Dough:

1 cup warm water
4 TBSP melted unsalted butter
1tsp sugar substitute
1 package quick rising yeast
3 cups whole wheat flour (may do ½ whole wheat, ½ white)
Splash of salt
1/3 cup agave nectar (may use honey)
1 egg, beaten

- Dissolve yeast and sugar in ½ cup warm water.
- Add butter, honey, salt, egg, remaining ½ cup water, and 1 cup of flour. Beat for 5 minutes on medium speed.
- Add remaining flour; beat for 5 minutes more.
- Let dough rise until doubled (at least 1-2 hours).

Filling:

1/2 cup brown sugar substitute (see conversion chart)
1/2 cup sugar substitute (see conversion chart)
1/4 cup unsalted melted
1 1/2 TBSP cinnamon

- Place brown sugar, sugar, butter, and cinnamon in mixing bowl and mix until combined.
- Roll out dough in a large rectangle and cover with mixture.
- Roll up and cut into 1-1.5 inch rolls.
- Place in greased baking pan.
- Bake 375 for 20-25 minutes, or until golden brown. Let cool for 10 minutes and prepare icing.

Icing:

Powdered sugar (see recipe this section)
2 TBSP skim milk
½ TBSP melted butter
½ tsp pure vanilla extract

Mix all ingredients in small mixing bowl and drizzle over cooked cinnamon rolls.

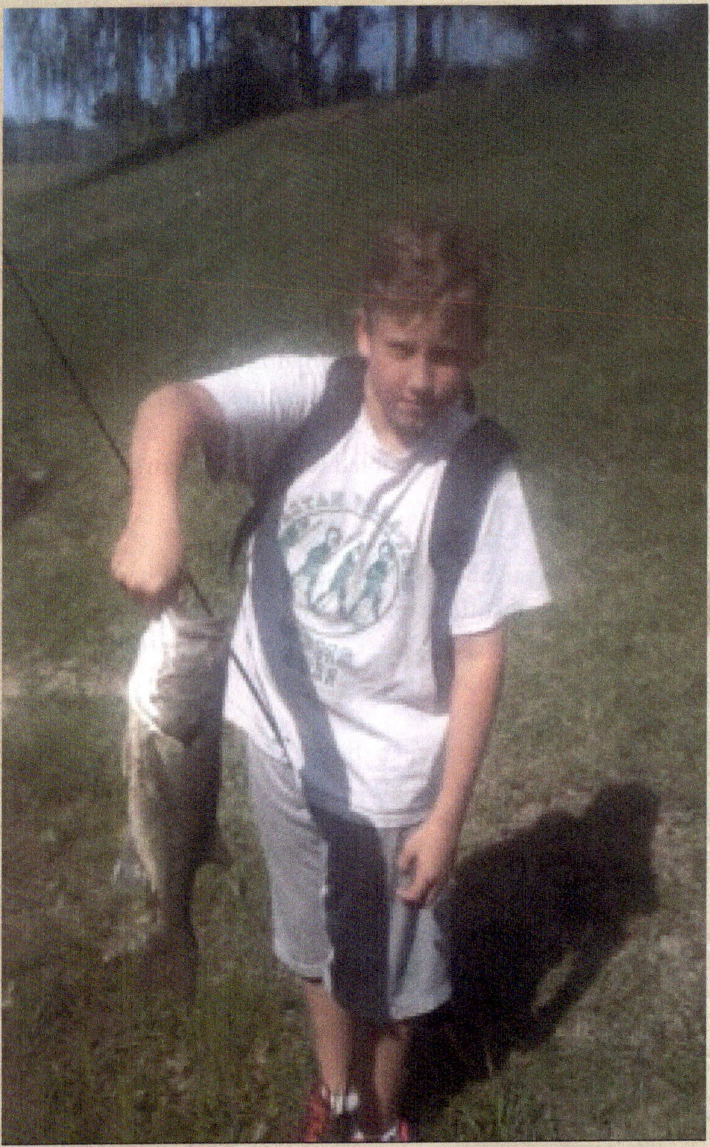

NANA'S CRANBERRY ORANGE BREAD

2 cups whole wheat flour (may do ½ whole wheat, ½ white)
Sugar substitute for 1 cup granulated sugar (see conversion chart)
½ cup milk
3TBSP vegetable oil (coconut or canola)
1 egg or 2 egg whites
2 tsp grated orange peel
¾ cup orange juice
1 tsp salt (omit if using self-rising flour)
3 ½ tsp baking powder (omit if using self-rising flour)
1 cup dried cranberries or fresh cranberries halved

- Preheat oven to 350.
- Mix all ingredients, except cranberries, in mixer on medium speed for 30 seconds scraping sides constantly. Add cranberries. Mix few more seconds until cranberries are blended in. *Bread will be rubbery if mix much longer than recommended mixing time.
- Pour bread mixture into greased and floured 9x5x3 baking loaf pan.
- Bake 50-60 min or until toothpick comes out clean from center.

Variation:
CRANBERRY-CHEDDAR BREAD
Serving size: 1/12 of loaf

1.5 tsp baking powder
½ tsp baking soda
½ tsp salt
2 TBSP unsalted butter
1.5 cups low fat shredded cheddar cheese
Allow to stand 8 hrs before slicing/eating.

Finisher
Little Rockers Kids Marathon
12229
LITTLE ROCK, AR
Today's THV 11
todaysthv.com

CREPES

Serving size: 1 crepe

1 can organic whole wheat prepared batter or any whole wheat pancake batter
½ TBSP powdered sugar (see recipe this section)
¼ cup favorite fruit or berry
Sugar free syrup or agave nectar

- Coat 6" skillet with cooking spray.
- Spray or spoon batter into skillet to create very thin circle leaving ½ -1 inch around border of skillet.
- Cook batter until cooked through flipping once.
- Place crepe on a plate and place favorite fruit or berries down the center.
- Roll crepe.
- Sprinkle powdered sugar (see recipe this section) on top and add syrup or agave nectar.

NOTE: *You can find the prepared batter in a can at Fresh Market or Whole Foods. My children really like the cinnamon and brown sugar flavor.*

FRITTATA

Servings: 4

3 egg whites + 3 whole eggs
2 TBSP skim milk
½ cup low fat cheese (cheddar, mozzarella, feta)
1 cup chopped vegetables of your choice
Pepper to taste

- Preheat oven to 425.
- Coat 8x8 baking dish or glass pie pan with nonstick vegetable cooking spray.
- Whisk eggs with milk in medium bowl.
- Add rest of ingredients and combine.
- Pour mixture into dish and bake 20 min. Let stand 5 minutes.

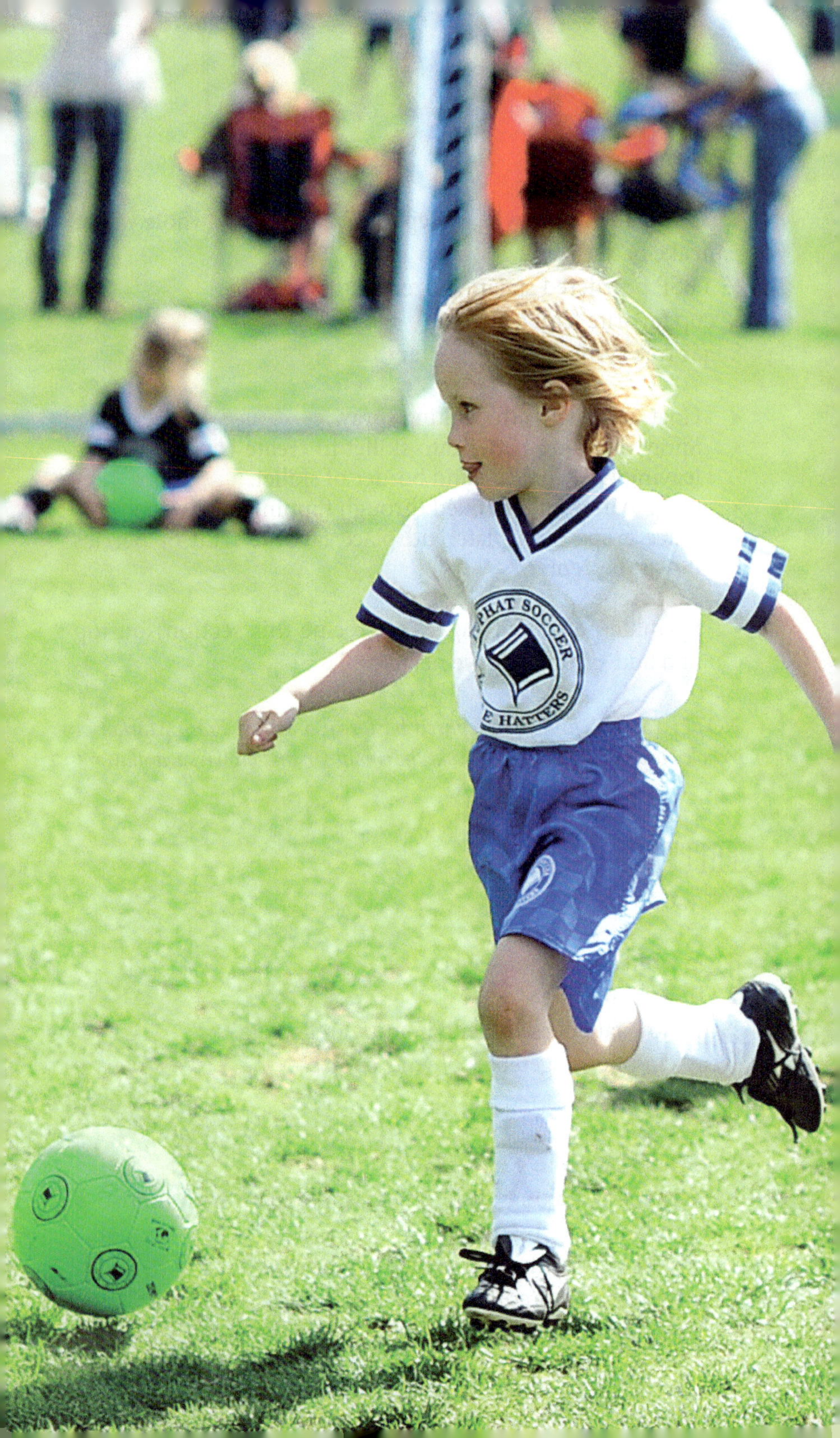

GARLIC PARMESAN TOAST

4 slices whole wheat bread
2 TBSP butter melted
1 TBSP minced garlic
Grated parmesan cheese

Stir minced garlic into melted butter and brush on wheat bread. Sprinkle piece with parmesan cheese. Broil in oven until toasted.

GRANOLA PARFAIT

½ cup unsweetened granola
Drizzle of honey or agave nectar
6 oz greek yogurt (of your choice)
½ cup fresh fruit or berries

- Drizzle honey or agave nectar over granola and stir until granola is coated.
- Layer granola, fruit, and yogurt to your preference.

MUFFINS
Makes 12 muffins

A running theme when researching "healthy" muffins was the use of wheat flour, oats, applesauce, and yogurt to replace "unhealthy ingredients." I used these basics and tweaked to the desired flavor. Recipe also inspired by the www.sundaybaker.com

1.5 cups quick cook oatmeal or old fashioned oats
½ cup whole wheat flour
1 (6 oz.) container Greek Yogurt (Flavor will vary. See below.)
1/2 c. pure maple syrup or agave nectar
1/2 c. unsweetened applesauce

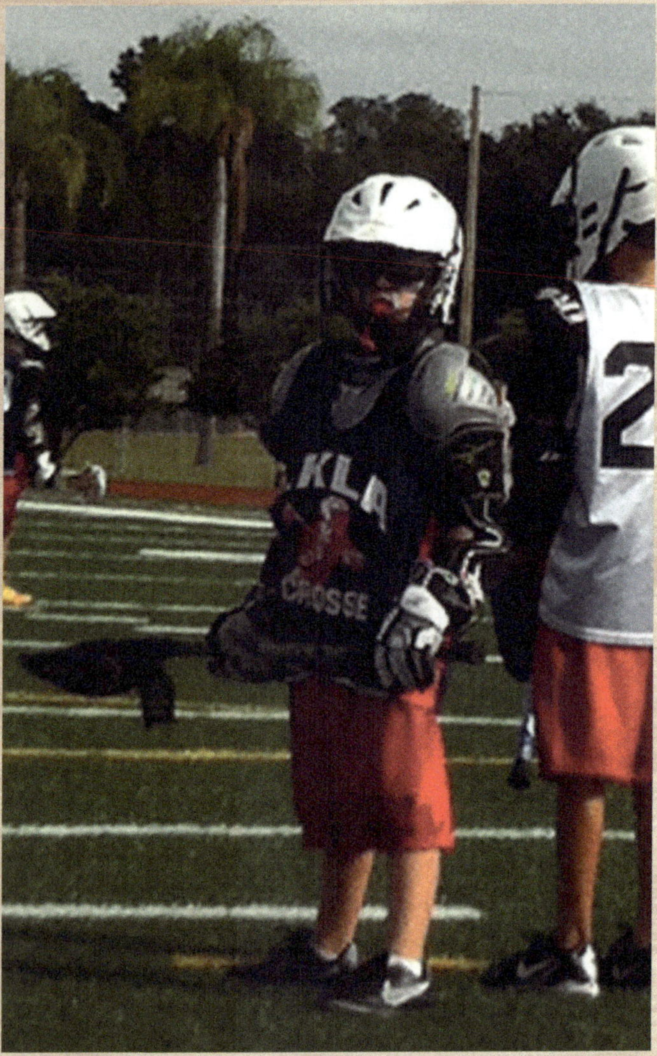

1 whole egg, 1 egg white
1-1/2 t. baking soda
1/2 t. baking powder

- Preheat oven to 375.
- Spray muffin tins with cooking spray.
- Mix all ingredients in food processor/blender until becomes a batter.
- Pour batter into large bowl and gently stir in fruit.
- Spoon the batter into the muffin tins ¾ full.
- Bake for 15 minutes, or until tops start to brown.

Blueberry
Follow basic muffin recipe with following variations:
- Vanilla or blueberry yogurt
- 1 cup fresh blueberries

Carrot
Follow basic muffin recipe with following variations:
- Vanilla yogurt
- 1 cup grated carrot
- 2 TBSP brown sugar substitute

Chocolate Chip
Follow basic muffin recipe with the following variations:
- Vanilla yogurt
- 1 cup healthy chocolate chips (sugar free, nondairy, etc)

Cranberry
Follow basic muffin recipe with the following variations:
- Blackberry or vanilla yogurt
- One cup fresh or dried cranberries

Nana's Fruit in the Center
- Fill muffin tins 1/2 full with muffin batter.
- Put 1 tsp sugar free fruit preserves (flavor your choice) in the

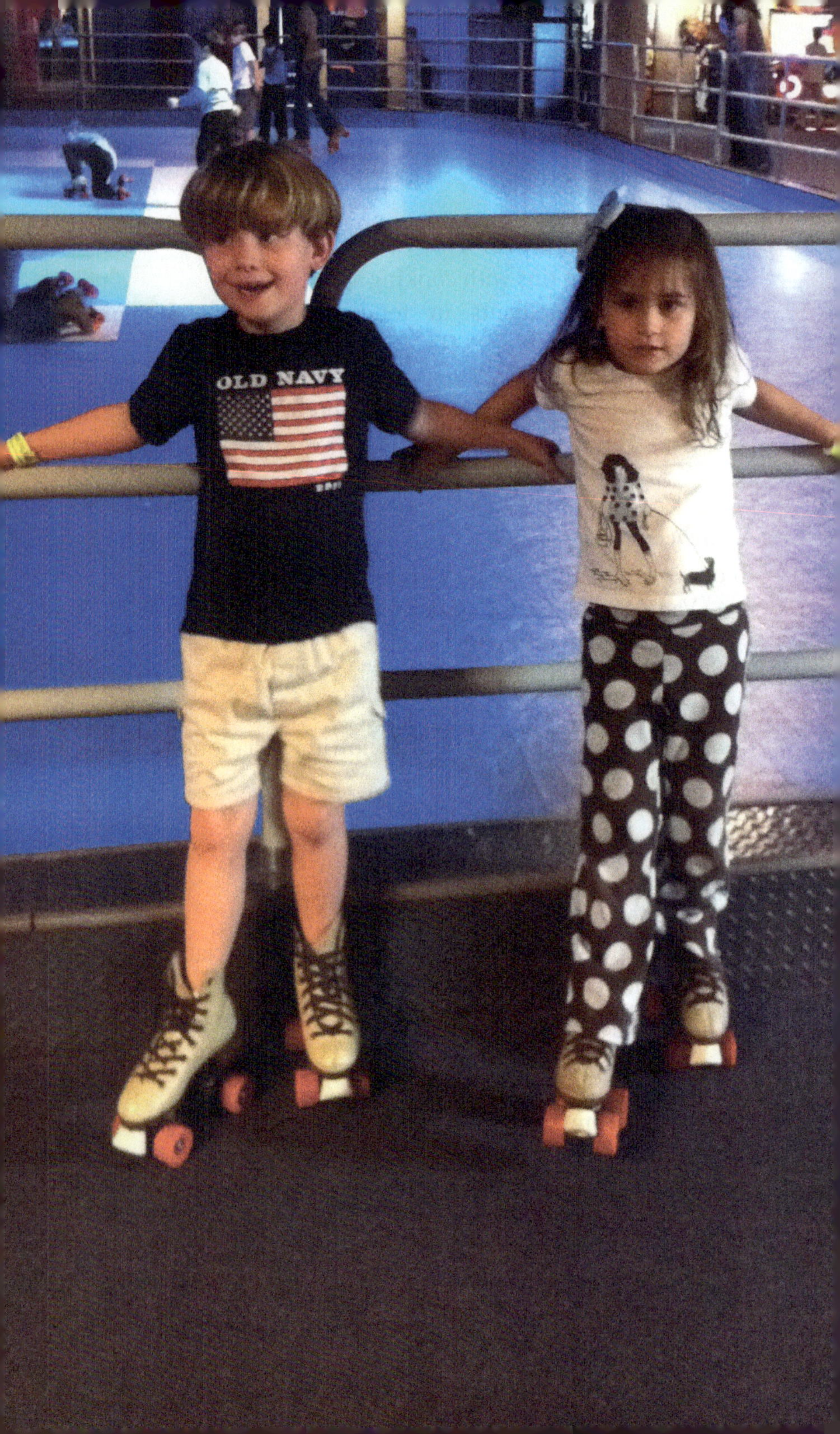
OLD NAVY

center of first layer batter.
- Pour remaining half of batter to fill the muffin tin.

"Plain"
- Use vanilla yogurt
- Add 2tsp vanilla
- Add 2tsp cinnamon
- Add 1TBSP brown sugar substitute

Strawberry
- Strawberry yogurt
- One cup sliced strawberries

POWDERED SUGAR

- 1 cup Xylitol or granulated Splenda
- 1-2 TBSP corn starch
- Blend sugar in corn starch in a blender until resembles powdered sugar.

REESE'S TOAST

1 piece whole wheat bread toasted
½ TBSP Natural Peanut Butter or PB2 Crunch
½ TBSP Nutella alternative (see recipe below)

Spread peanut butter on toast. Spread "nutella" on top of peanut butter.

NUTELLA

1 TBSP cocoa
1 TBSP honey or agave nectar (I prefer)
1 TBSP coconut oil

Mix all together.

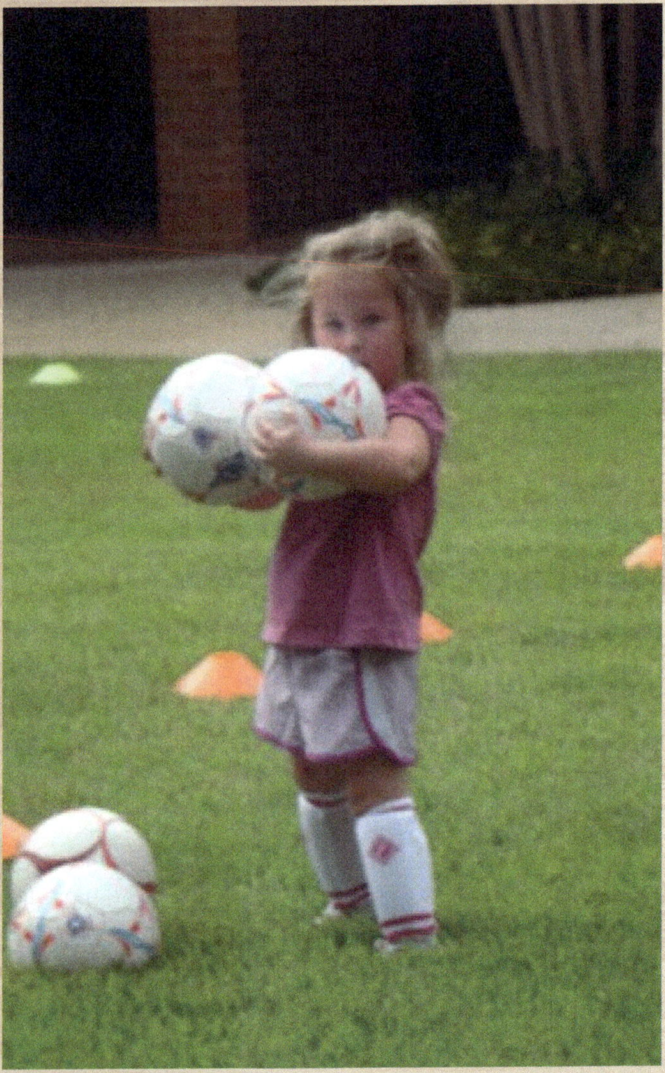

SCONES

1 ½ cups whole wheat flour (may do ½ whole wheat, ½ white)
2 tsp baking powder
4 TBSP cold unsalted butter
Sugar substitute for 2 TBSP sugar (see conversion chart)
1 egg beaten or 2 egg whites beaten
Add to skim milk to egg to make equal parts.

- Preheat oven 425.
- Sift flour and baking powder into mixing bowl.
- Add butter and sugar mix on low speed.
- Add in eggs/milk mixture and mix all until forms a soft dough (not sticky).
- Place dough on floured working board and roll out to ½ inch thickness.
- Cut dough with 2" round or triangle cookie cutter and place on floured baking sheet.
- Bake 425 for 12-15 minutes or until golden brown.

May add: 1 cup cranberries, raisins, blueberries, chocolate chips, etc.

WHOLE WHEAT PASTRIES

2 1/4 cups whole wheat pastry flour OR if cannot find whole wheat pastry flour, use 1 cup whole wheat flour and 1 cup white pastry flour (will last longer if use both)
1/2 teaspoons salt
Sugar substitute for 1 TSBP sugar (see conversion chart)
1 stick cold unsalted butter, cut into 1/2-inch cubes
1 egg, slightly beaten
Ice water

- In a food processor/blender, pulse together flour, salt, and sugar.
- Add in the butter. Pulse a few times until the mixture is crumbly.

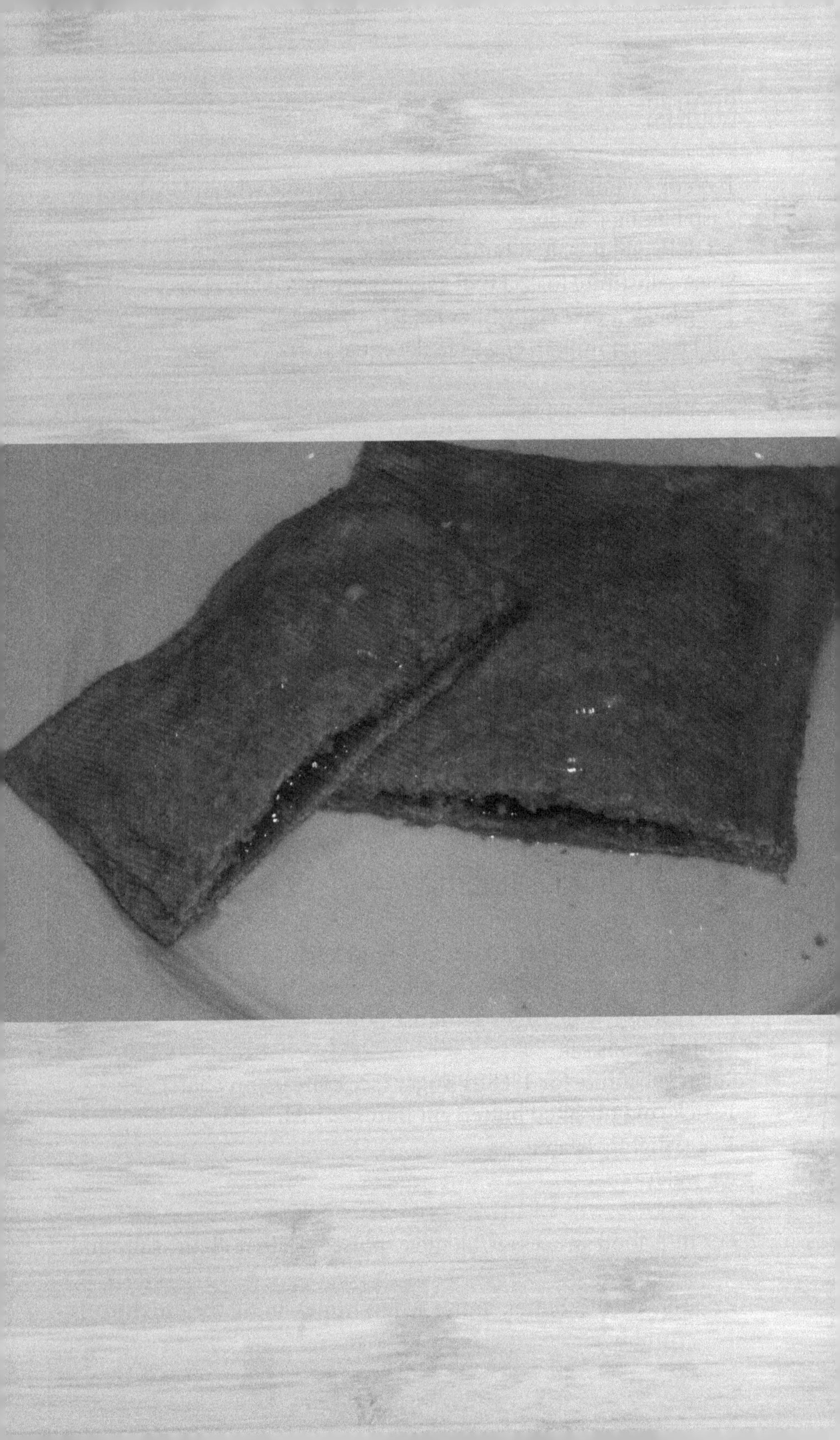

- Combine the egg and water in a small bowl.
- Pour the water/egg mixture in and pulse until mixture just comes together.
- Pour mixture out onto a floured board and knead a few times to blend all the ingredients together.
- If freezing, double wrap in plastic wrap and freeze for later.

POP TARTS

Above recipe + Sugar free fruit preserves

- Preheat oven to 375.
- Sprinkle flour onto working surface and roll out dough.
- Cut into 4x5 rectangles (cut only as many as you think you will need).
- Place rectangle on baking sheet lined with wax paper.
- Put 1 TSBP preserves in center of rectangle.
- Cover with matching rectangle and press seams together with a fork.
- Bake 375 for 12-15 minutes.

Icing:
1-2 cups powdered sugar
¼ cup boiling water
1 TBSP butter

Once water is boiling, remove from heat. Add butter. Stir in powdered sugar until achieve desired consistency. Drizzle over pop tarts.

TURNOVERS
(Grandmama's Fried Pies)

Above recipe for pastry

Filling:
Choice of Fruit:

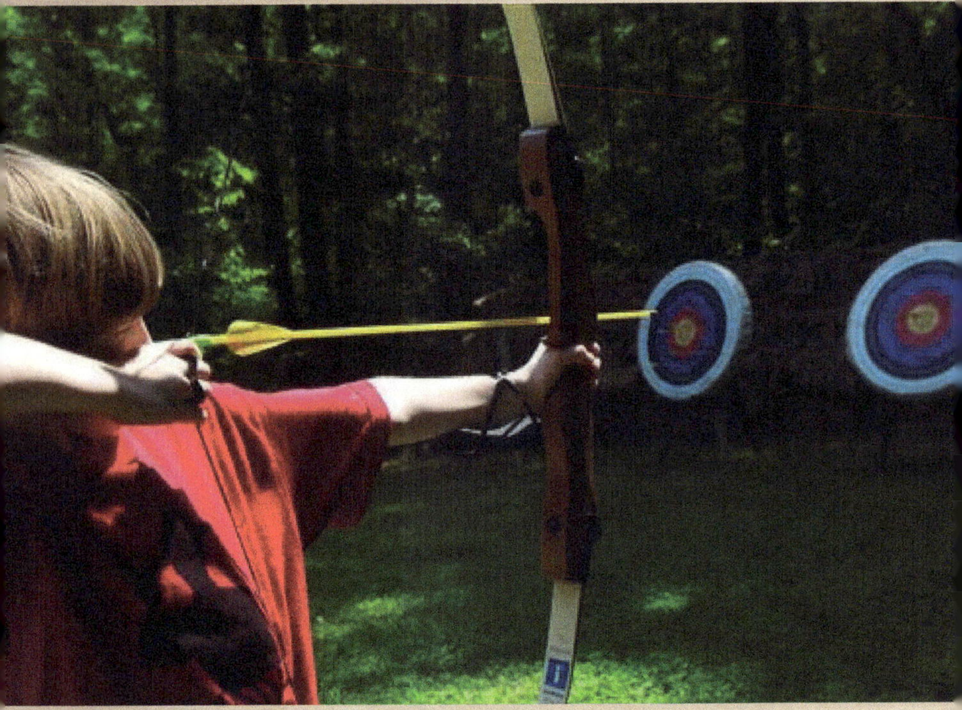

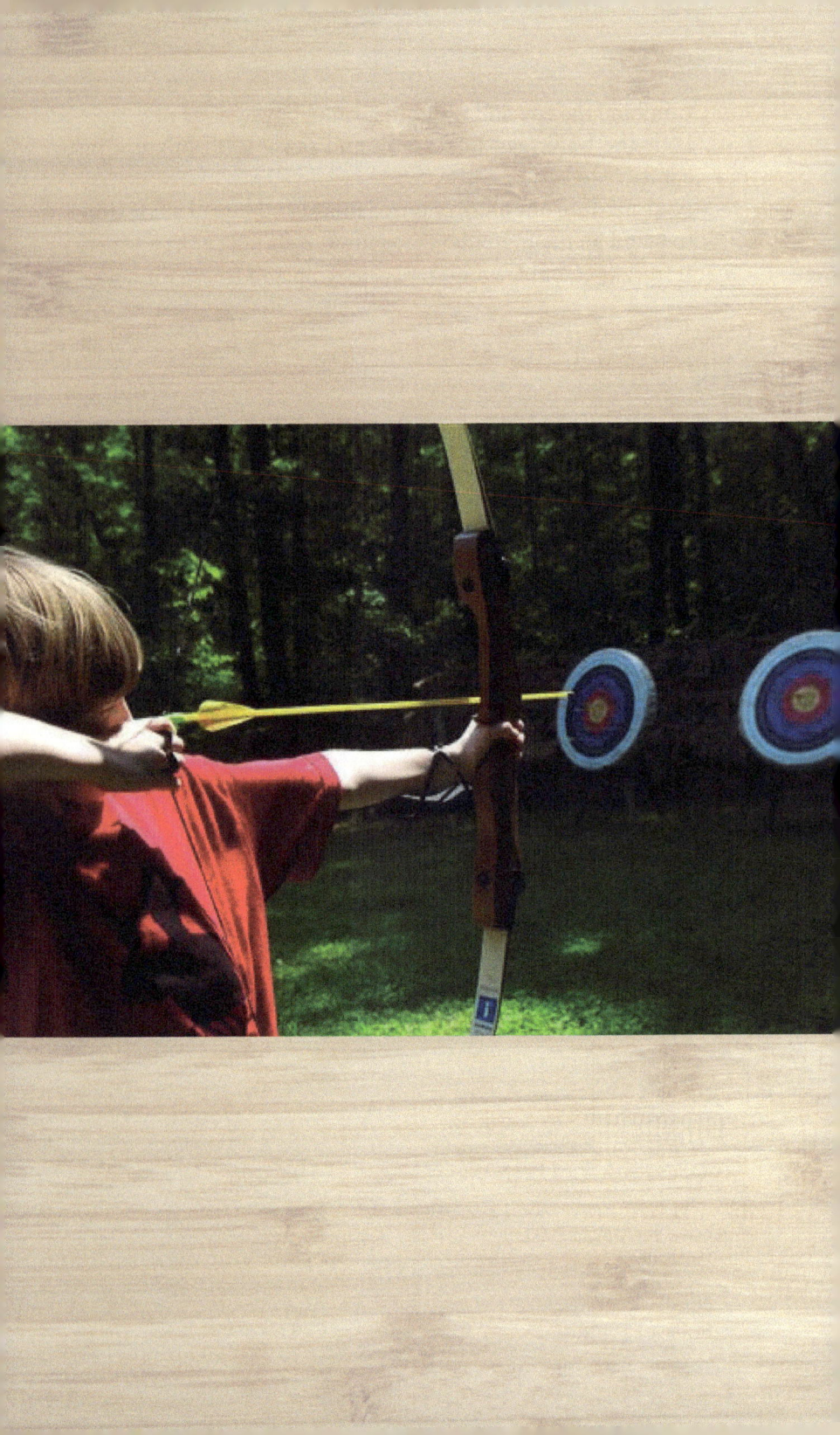

3 granny smith apples peeled and grated OR
3 large peaches peeled and grated OR
3 large pears peeled and grated OR
Sugar substitute for 3 TBSP sugar (see conversion chart)
1/2 teaspoon cinnamon
1/4 teaspoon fresh lemon juice
1 tablespoon honey
Unsalted butter

- Preheat oven to 400.
- Combine fruit and next four ingredients.
- On floured working surface, roll out dough and cut into 4x4 squares.
- Place spoonful of fruit mixture in center of square and top with 1tsp unsalted butter.
- Fold dough corner to corner to resemble triangle.
- Press seams with a fork to seal.
- May sprinkle/brush tops with sugar substitute and cinnamon.
- Bake 400 for 20 minutes or until start to brown.

NANA'S ZUCCHINI BREAD

Serving size: 1/12 of loaf

Dry Ingredients:
1.5 cups whole wheat flour
Sugar substitute for ¾ cup sugar
¼ tsp baking soda
¼ tsp salt
1.5 tsp cinnamon

Wet Ingredients:
2 eggs or 4 egg whites
2 large zucchini (mashed)
¼ cup oil
1.5 tsp vanilla

- Preheat oven to 350.
- Mix dry ingredients. If using a liquid sugar substitute, still use in "dry" list.
- Mix wet ingredients. (I put the zucchini in a food processor/blender.)
- Mix dry and wet ingredients together in large bowl.
- Add to greased 9x5x3 loaf pan.
- Bake for 40 minutes or until toothpick comes out clean from the center.

3
SOUPS

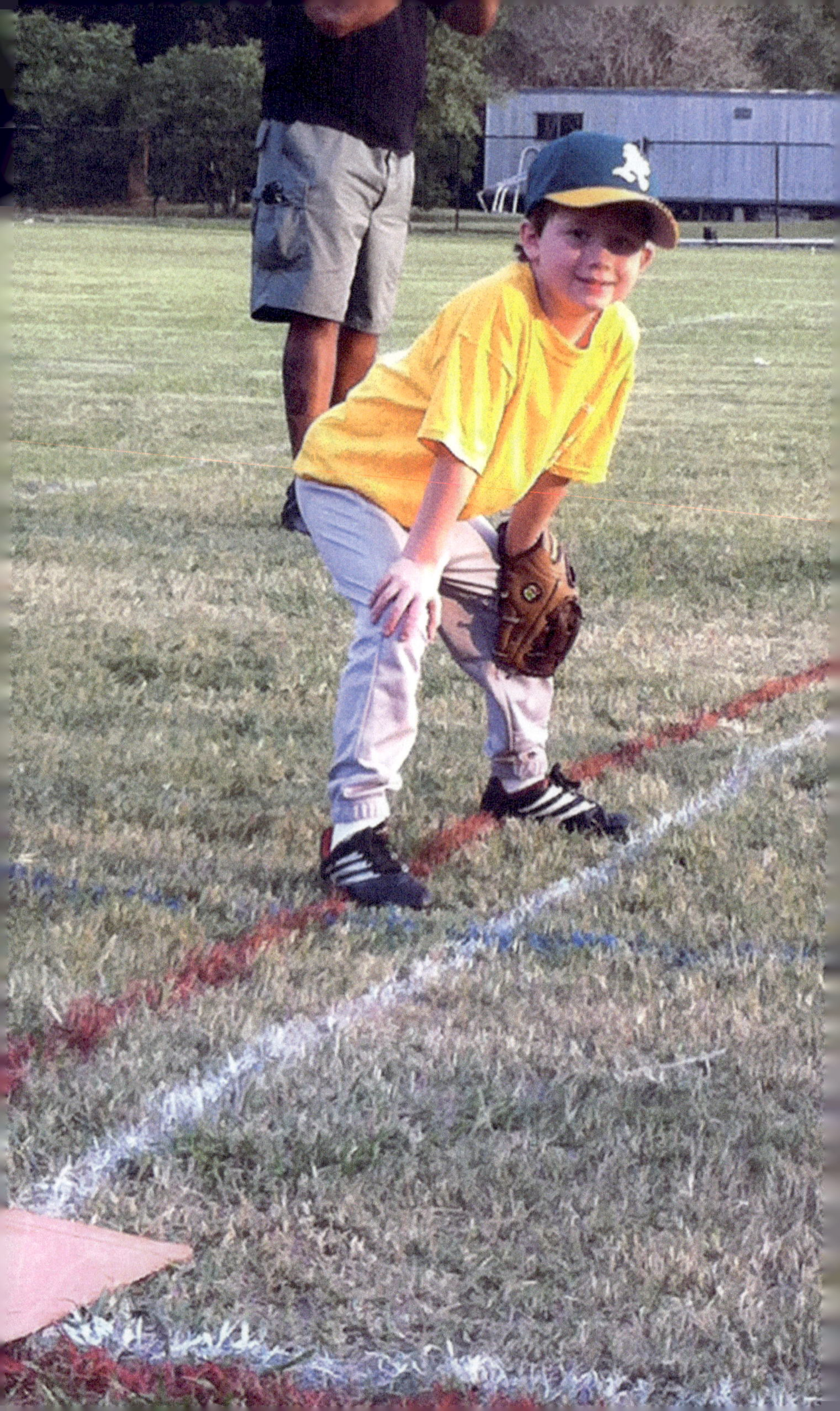

BUTTERNUT SQUASH & GREEN APPLE SOUP

Makes 4 servings. Serving size: 1 cup
Inspired by our favorite from Fresh Market

1 large Butternut Squash peeled and cubed (Hint: some grocery stores sell butternut squash already cubed)
3 Granny Smith apples, peeled and sliced
1 TBSP nutmeg
4 cups fat free, low-sodium chicken broth
2 TBSP heavy cream (optional for creamier texture)
Salt and pepper to taste

- In large pot, boil butternut squash and apples in chicken broth until tender.
- Puree in food processor/blender. Return to pot.
- Add nutmeg.
- Add cream (optional).
- Keep warm until ready to serve.

CARROT SOUP

Makes 6 servings. Serving size: 1 cup

1.5 lbs carrots cut in chunks
6 cups vegetable broth
2 TBSP light, salted butter
1 TBSP brown sugar substitute (refer to conversion chart)
Salt and freshly ground pepper to taste

- In large pot, boil carrots in chicken broth until soft.
- Place boiled carrots, broth, butter, and brown sugar in food processor/blender and puree. Return to pot.
- Add salt and pepper to taste.
- May add more brown sugar substitute to taste.

Keep warm until ready to serve.

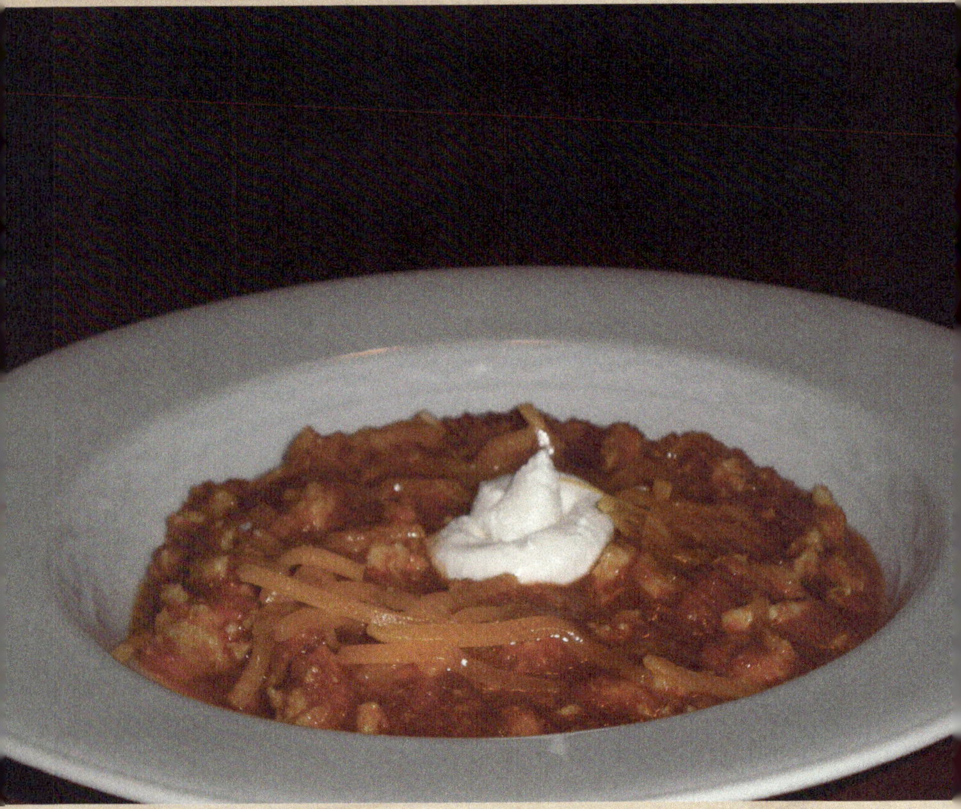

CHICKEN NOODLE SOUP
Makes 6 servings. Serving size: 1 cup

2 cups whole wheat rotini
4 cups low sodium, fat free chicken broth
2 cups rotisserie chicken pieces (or 2 baked chicken breasts cubed)
Salt and pepper to taste
*optional – add vegetables such as diced carrots, peas, or celery

- Cook whole wheat rotini according to package directions and drain.
- Place all ingredients in pot.
- Heat soup on low-medium heat until all ingredients are warmed together. If add vegetables, heat until veggies soften.

CHILI
Serving size: 1 cup
My children usually go for "seconds" which is fine with me!

1 lb ground breast of turkey, cooked and drained
1 packet Chili-O chili seasoning
3 cups low sodium, fat-free chicken broth

Vegetables:
2 carrots peeled and cut into chunks
1 red bell pepper seeded and cut into chunks
1 zucchini peeled and cut into chunks
1 28oz can diced tomatoes
1 can kidney beans drained (optional)
½ cup chopped onion (optional)

- Bring broth to boil in large pot. Add chosen vegetables (except tomatoes, beans, and onion). Boil until soft.
- While vegetables are boiling, brown ground turkey breast

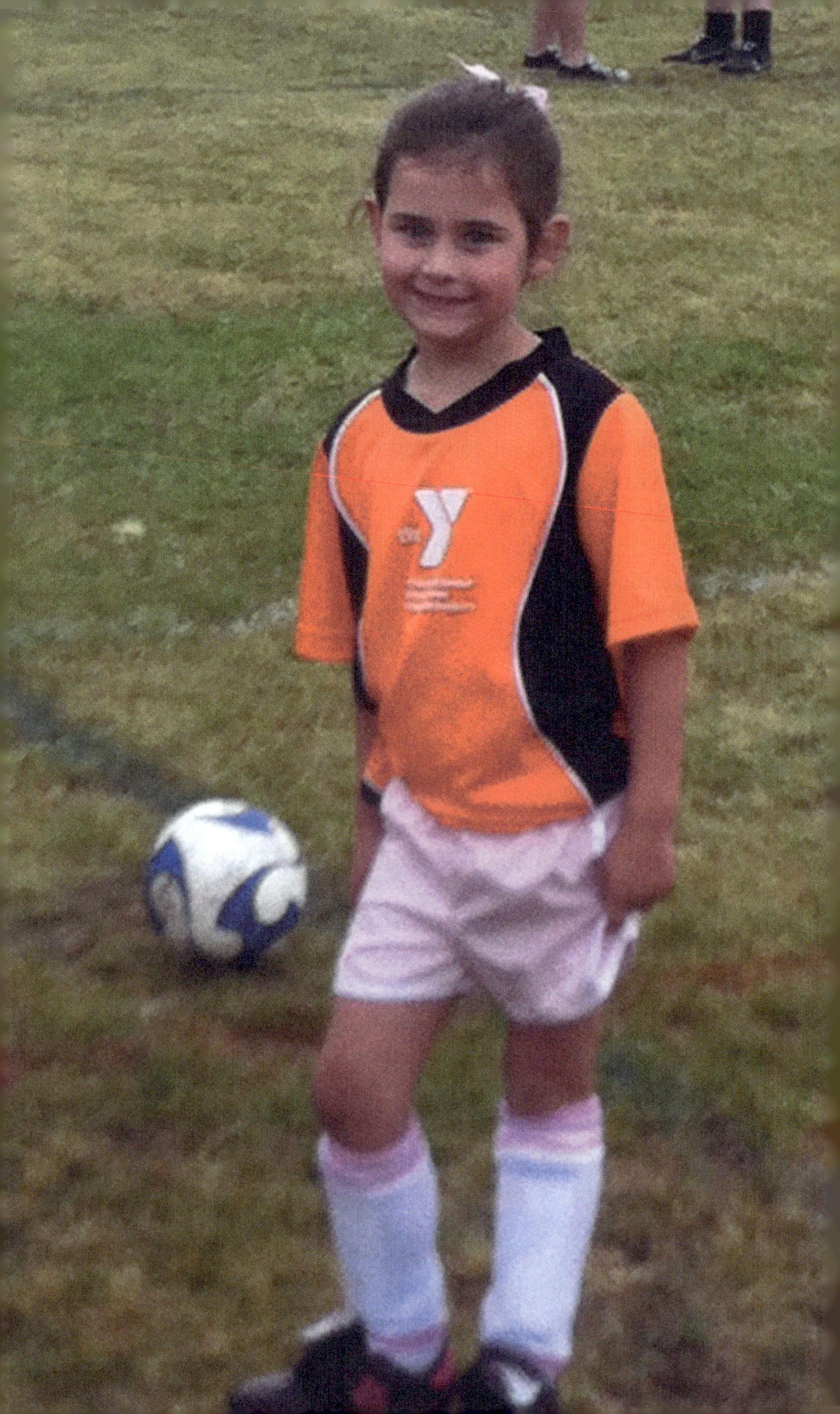

in large skillet. Drain if needed. Set aside.
- Drain vegetables. Place in food processor/blender with diced tomatoes. Process until resembles a "rough" textured sauce. You may have to do in batches.
- Pour ground breast of turkey and pureed vegetables in large pot. Stir in Chili-O. Stir in chopped onion and beans if choose to.
- Heat on low-medium heat about 10-15 minutes, stirring occasionally until all ingredients heated through.

*Garnish with a dollup of fat free sour cream and/or a sprinkle of low fat shredded cheddar.

CORN CHOWDER
Serving size: 1 cup

2 cups cauliflower
½ cup onion
3 ears fresh corn (or 2 cans)
3 cups fat free low sodium chicken broth
1 cup red bell pepper diced (optional)
1 cup diced carrots (fresh or can)
4 slices turkey bacon, cooked and crumbled
Salt and pepper to taste
½ cup heavy cream (optional)

- In large pot, boil cauliflower and onion in broth until tender.
- Remove cauliflower and 1/4 cup broth and puree in food processor. Return mixture to pot with chicken broth.
- Add remaining ingredients to pot and heat through.

For White Chicken Chili: use above recipe excluding bacon. Add 1 can diced green chiles. Add 2 cups rotisserie chicken pieces.

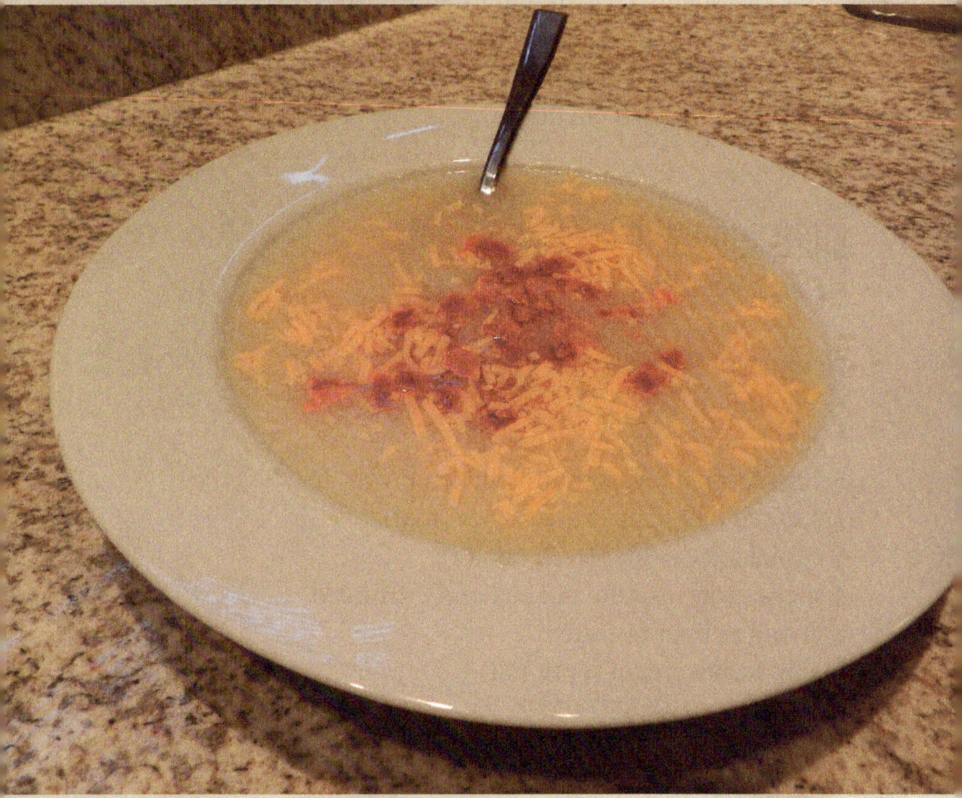

POTATO SOUP

Makes 8 servings. Serving size: 1 cup

1 head cauliflower with florets removed from stem
Small onion
3 cups fat free, low sodium chicken broth
3 slices turkey bacon cooked and crumbled
3 TBSP light salted butter
½ cup heavy cream
Low fat shredded cheddar
Salt and Pepper to taste

- Boil cauliflower and onion in chicken broth.
- Place boiled cauliflower, onion and broth into food processor. Add butter and cream and pulse.
- Salt and pepper to taste.
- Sprinkle servings with bacon crumbles and cheese.

TORTILLA SOUP

Makes 6 servings. Serving: 1 cup

Kernels from 3 ears fresh corn (or canned corn)
4 cups low sodium, fat free chicken broth
2 cups rotisserie chicken pieces (1 can chunk chicken)
1 15oz can black beans (my children won't eat black beans so we eliminate)
1 10oz can diced Rotel
Low fat shredded cheddar
Fat-free sour cream

Put all ingredients in large pot on medium heat 15-20 minutes stirring occasionally. Sprinkle each serving of soup with shredded cheddar and a dollup of sour cream.

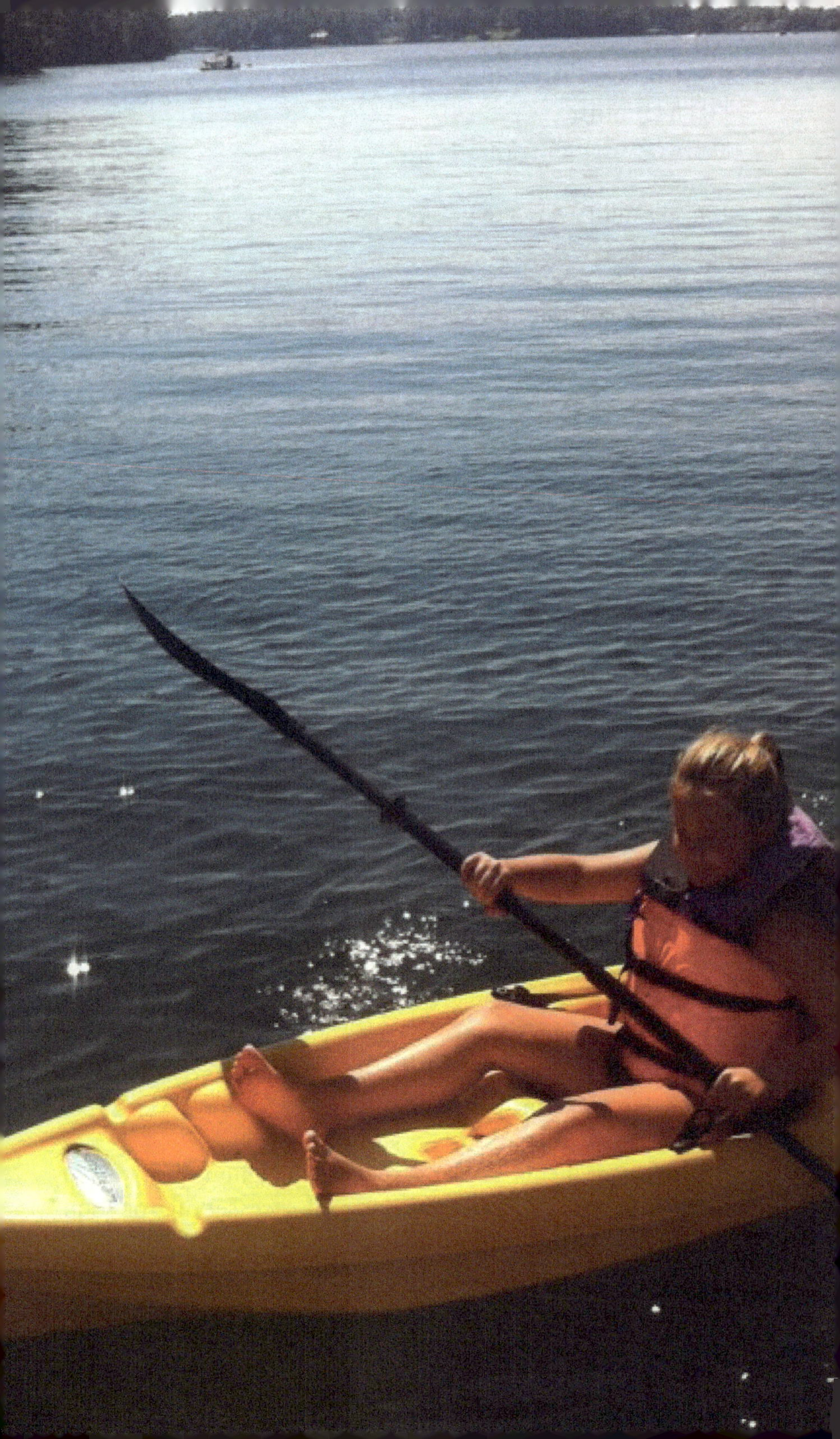

VEGETABLE SOUP

Serving size: 1 cup

4 cups fat free, low sodium beef broth
1 bag frozen mixed vegetables (or use comparable fresh vegetables diced)
2 cups Lean flank steak or tofu (cubed)

Cook all ingredients in large pot until meat is done.

MEALS

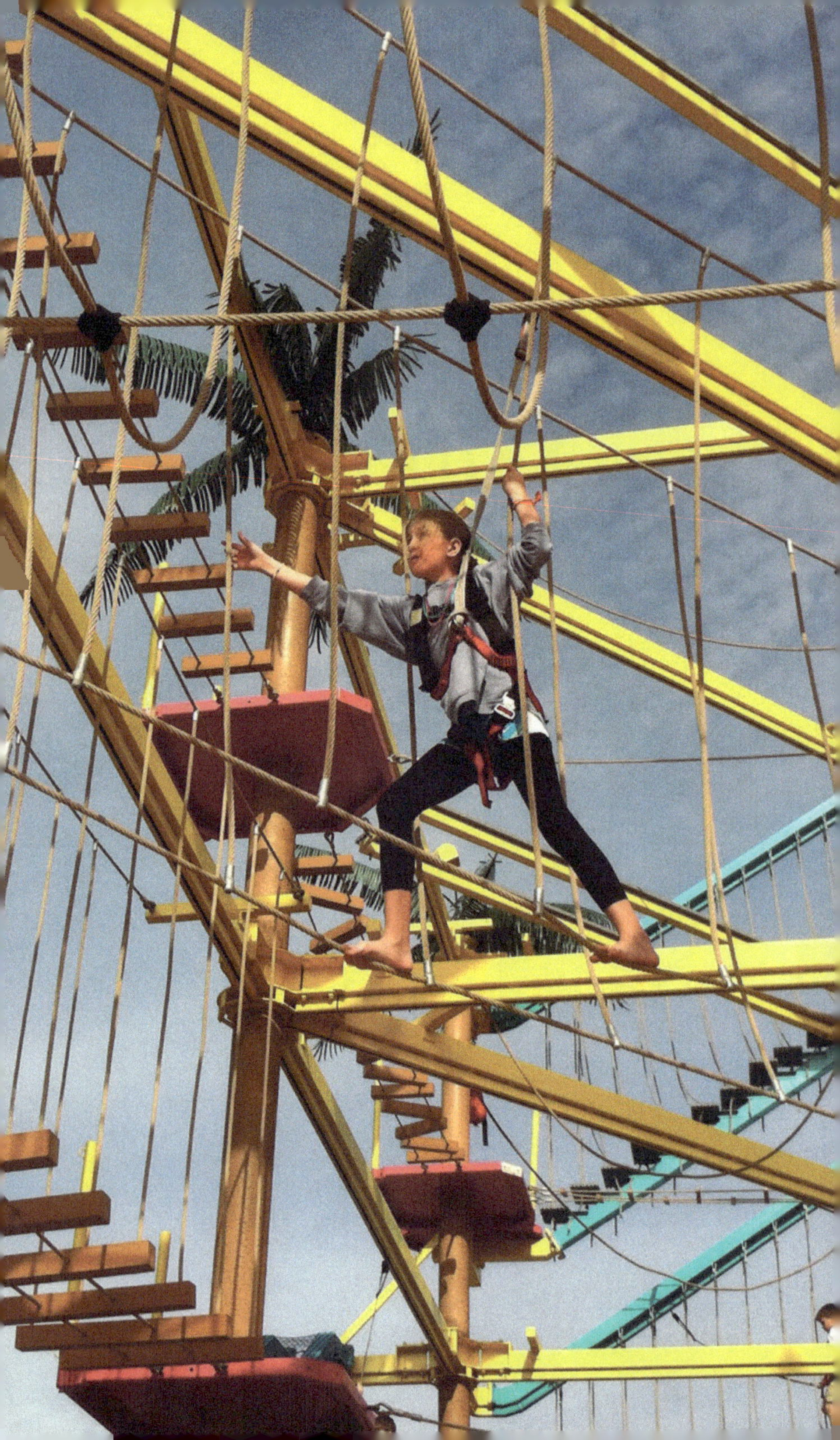

A BALANCED DINNER EXAMPLE

(refer to the portion chart for portion sizes OR use your portion plate)

Protein	Starch	Vegetables	Milk	Fruit
Examples: Fish, lean red meat, chicken, turkey	**Examples:** Corn, potatoes, rice, pasta, bread *Avoid "2nds" in this category	**Examples:** Green leafy vegetables, carrots, broccoli, salad, grilled vegetables, vegetables drizzled with fat-free dressing, etc *if children want "2nds," encourage them from this category	**Examples:** Yogurt, cheese, sour cream, fat free milk, etc.	**Examples:** Apple slices, berries, melon, grapes, orange slices, mango, pineapple, etc.

Below is what your meal portions should look like. Plate coming soon to www.kickinitkids.com

69

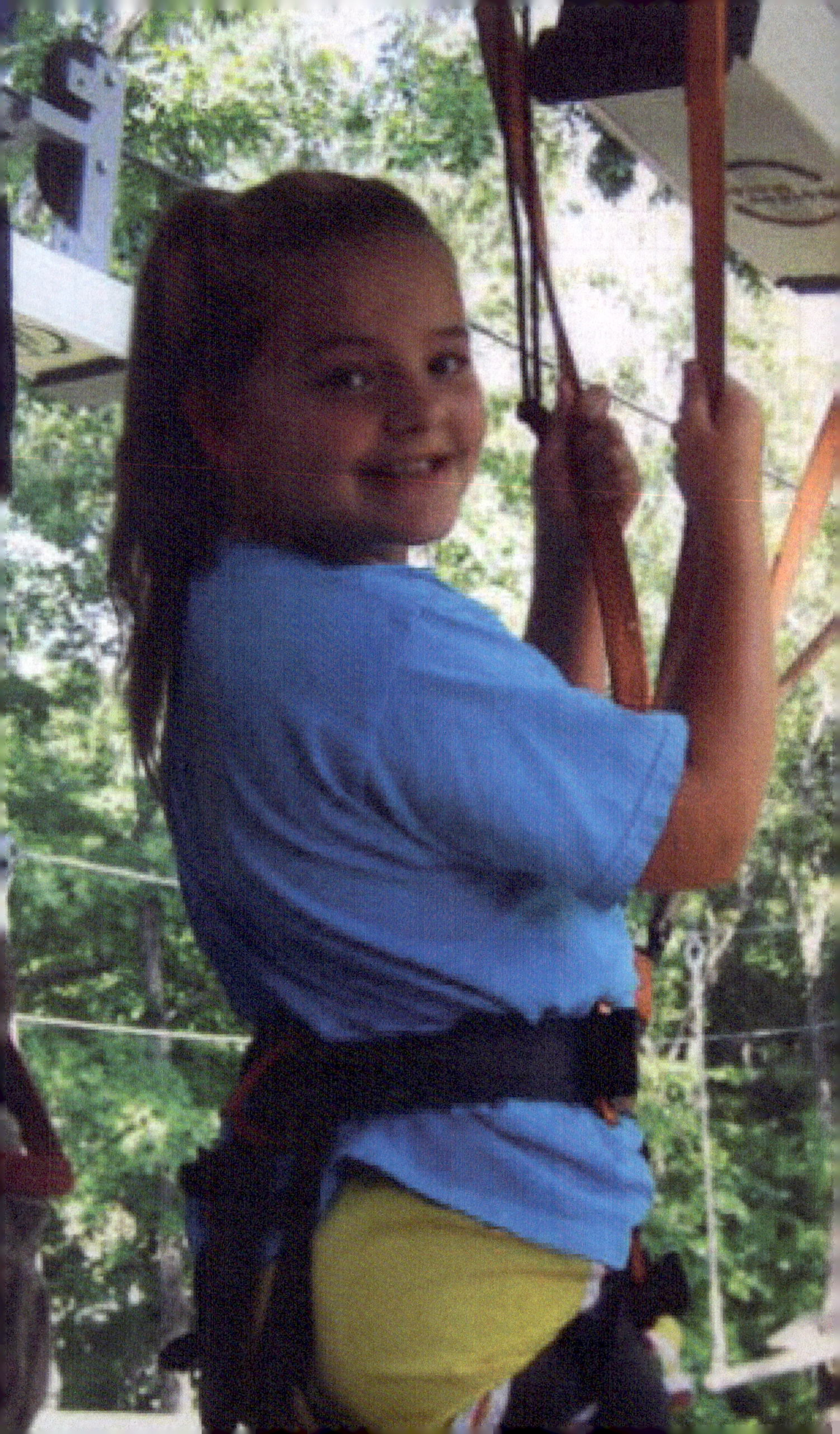

The following are the recipes I use when my family needs a variation to the "balanced meal" dinners.

TIPS

- Do yourself a favor!! Keep aluminum foil baking pans or Tupperware on hand for freezing dinners. Almost every meal is a freezable meal. Make extra and freeze! You will thank yourself. Cover meal with plastic wrap, and press on top of meal sealing. Cover plastic wrap with foil. Again, press foil tightly against meal and seal edges. Label and date.
- Freeze sauces in tupperware containers.
- Wrap pastry dough in plastic wrap and freeze.
- If your child has other "favorites," use the information I have given you and transform any meal! Of course, the internet has tons of guiding resources as well.

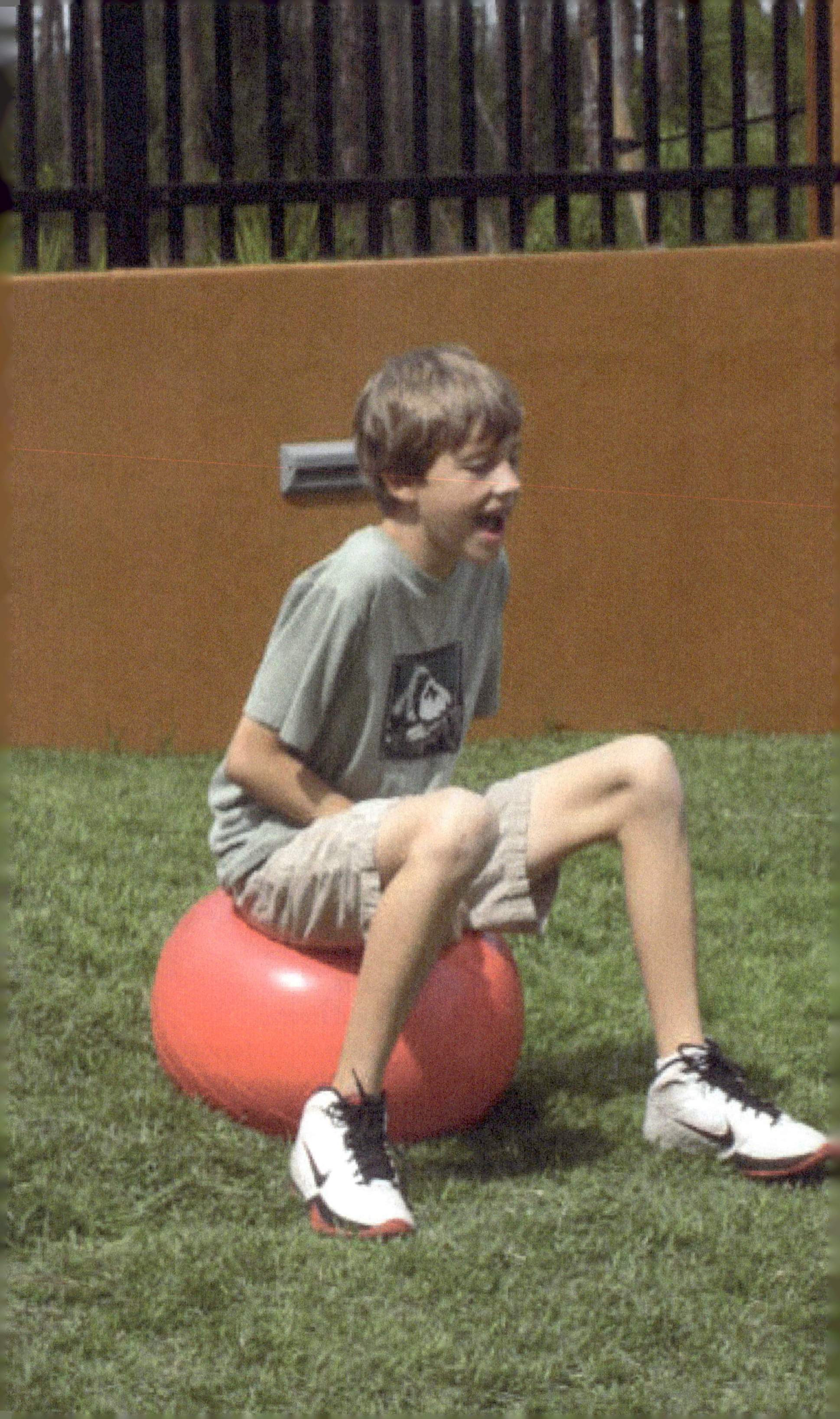

ANNIE'S CHICKEN TENDERS

Nonstick cooking spray
4 chicken breasts cut into ½" strips
4 cups brown rice crispy cereal
¼ tsp salt
1.5 cups whole wheat flour
2 eggs beaten
1/4 cup lowfat or skim milk

- Preheat oven to 425. Place a wire rack on a baking sheet and lightly mist with nonstick cooking spray.
- Put cereal in gallon Ziploc bag and crush to about a cup.
- In a shallow bowl combine cereal with salt and pepper.
- In a second shallow bowl, beat egg whites with milk.
- Place flour in a third shallow bowl.
- Coat each chicken tender with flour shaking off excess.
- Coat each flour coated tender in egg mixture.
- Lastly, coat in cereal.
- Place on rack on baking sheet and mist chicken with cooking spray.
- Bake 18-20 min or until crust is golden brown.

Dipping Sauce Suggestions:
Fat free honey mustard dressing
Fat free ranch dressing
Low fat sesame ginger dressing

BAKED HERBED CHEESE & CHICKEN ROLL UPS

Serving size: 1 chicken breast with ½ cup rice (+ vegetables/salad)

4 chicken breasts – pound to ¼ inch thickness
Fat-free Italian dressing
8oz reduced fat cream cheese (tub works easiest)
2 TBSP Ranch dressing packet or Italian dressing packet

- Using a meat mallet, pound chicken in Ziploc bag until ¼ inch thick.
- Marinate chicken breasts in dressing at least one hour in gallon Ziploc bag.
- Mix dry dressing in tub of cream cheese until blended well. Put cream cheese in snack or sandwich ziploc. Squeeze it down to one corner and cut the corner off with scissors forming an "icing bag."

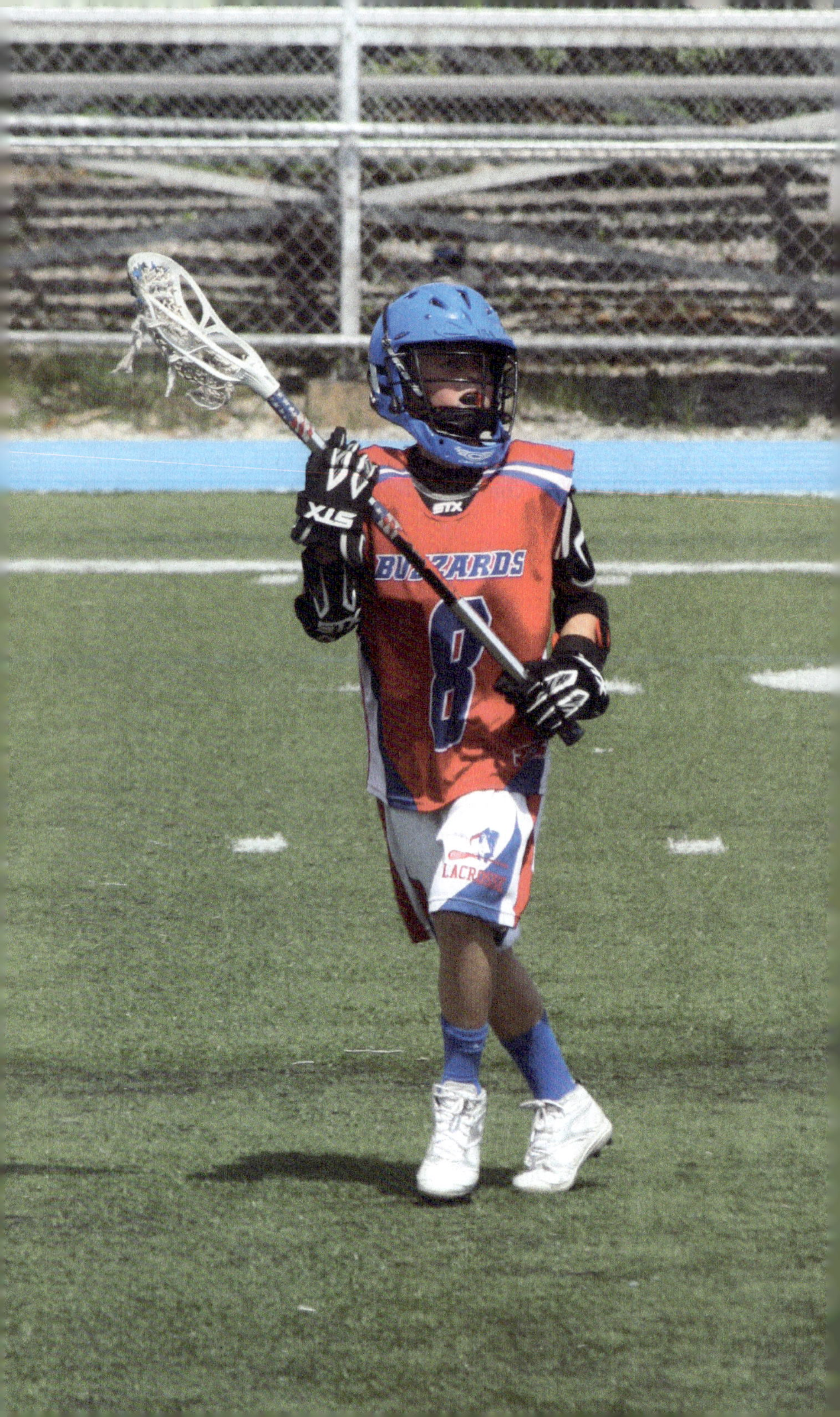
STX
8

- Place pounded chicken onto foil lined baking sheet. Squeeze two cream cheese parallel lines down center of each chicken breast.
- Roll each chicken breast and secure with a toothpick.
- Bake 350 for 30 minutes.

CABBAGE AND SAUSAGE

Makes 6-8 servings
Sarah 11, Shea 9, and Mary Scott 6

1 Head Cabbage cut in chunks
1 package Hillshire turkey sausage (or chicken sausage)
1 TBSP olive oil
½ cup water

- Put Olive oil in large skillet or wok over medium heat.
- Slice sausage and brown slightly in skillet/wok.
- Add cabbage to skillet/wok with turkey.
- Add water.
- Cover and steam for about an hour.

MISS DOTTIE'S CHICKEN CASSEROLE

Makes 8 servings. Serving size: 1 cup casserole over ½ cup rice or quinoa (+ vegetables/salad)

8 chicken breasts
1 can fat-free or low fat sour cream
1 can Campbells Healthy Request cream of chicken
2 cups cauliflower (optional –sneaky)
2 cups uncooked brown rice or quinoa (allow 25 minutes to cook)

- Bake chicken breasts at 350 on foil lined baking sheet for 30 minutes (until cooked through). Allow to cool.
- If using cauliflower, boil until tender while chicken is cooking. Puree boiled cauliflower and ½ can soup in blender/food processor.
- In large bowl, mix chopped chicken, sour cream and soup together (or cauliflower mixture and remaining soup).
- Pour into baking dish. Bake 350 for 20 minutes or until bubbly.
- While casserole is baking, cook brown rice or quinoa according to directions.

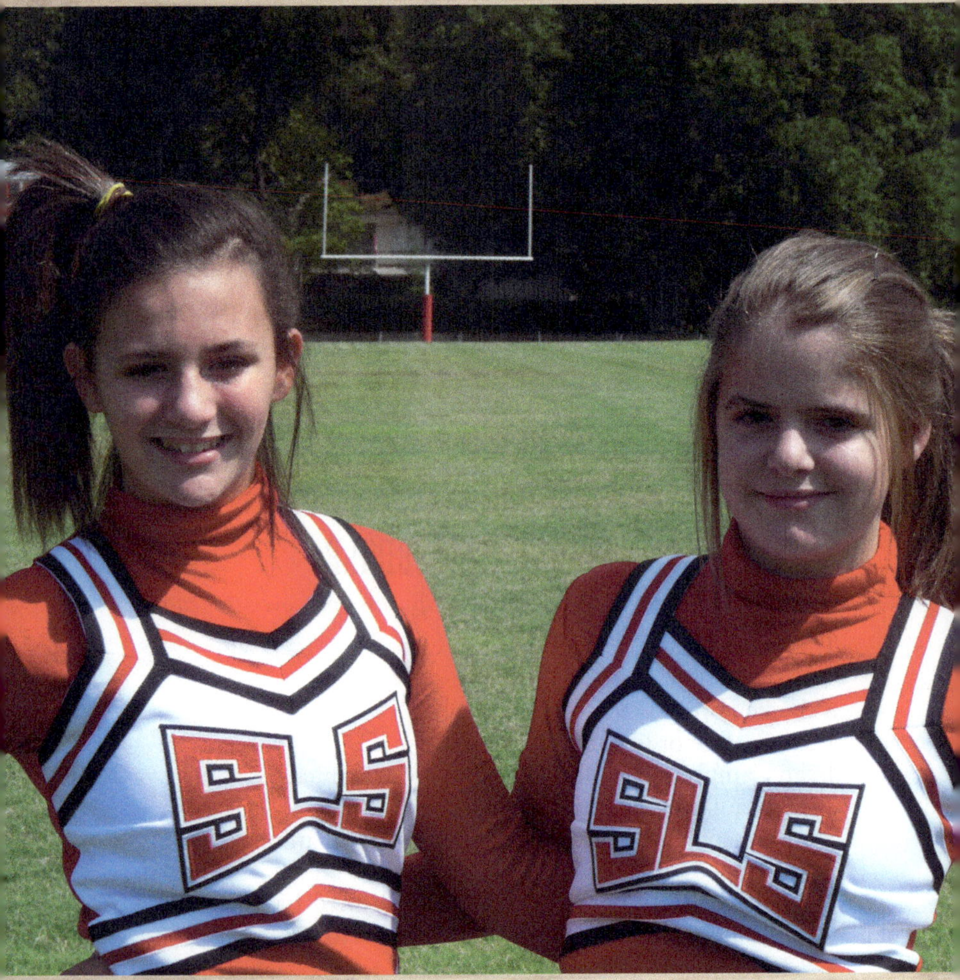
SLS
SLS

CHICKEN ENCHILADAS

Whole wheat tortillas
6 Chicken breasts
16 oz fat free or low fat sour cream
1 cup low fat shredded cheddar
1-2 TBSP canned diced green chiles (optional)
1 small can sliced black olives (optional)
Add additional veggies

Sauce:
1 can mild enchilada sauce
8oz lowfat or nonfat sour cream

- Bake chicken at 350 for 30-40 minutes and tear into pieces.
- Mix chicken pieces, 8oz sour cream, cheddar, chiles, black olives together in large bowl.
- In medium saucepan, heat enchilada sauce and sour cream together until sour cream is melted completely.
- Place 1/2 cup or so of chicken mixture down center of one whole wheat tortilla and roll up. You can use a toothpick to hold tortilla together or place fold side down.
- Place rolled enchiladas in 9x13 baking dish.
- Pour enchilada sauce evenly over enchiladas.
- Bake covered at 350 for 25-30 minutes.

CHICKEN PARMESAN

Serving size: 1 completed chicken breast (+ vegetables/salad)

4 chicken breasts
Whole wheat bread crumbs (if cannot find, toast 8-10 pieces whole wheat bread and crumble)
1 packet Italian dressing
2 whole eggs, 2 egg whites
Parmesan or low fat mozzarella (optional)
"Daddy's" marinara (see pg. 87)

- Make marinara.
- Preheat oven to 350.
- In shallow bowl, beat eggs gently until blended.
- In a different shallow bowl, mix bread crumbs and Italian dressing packet.

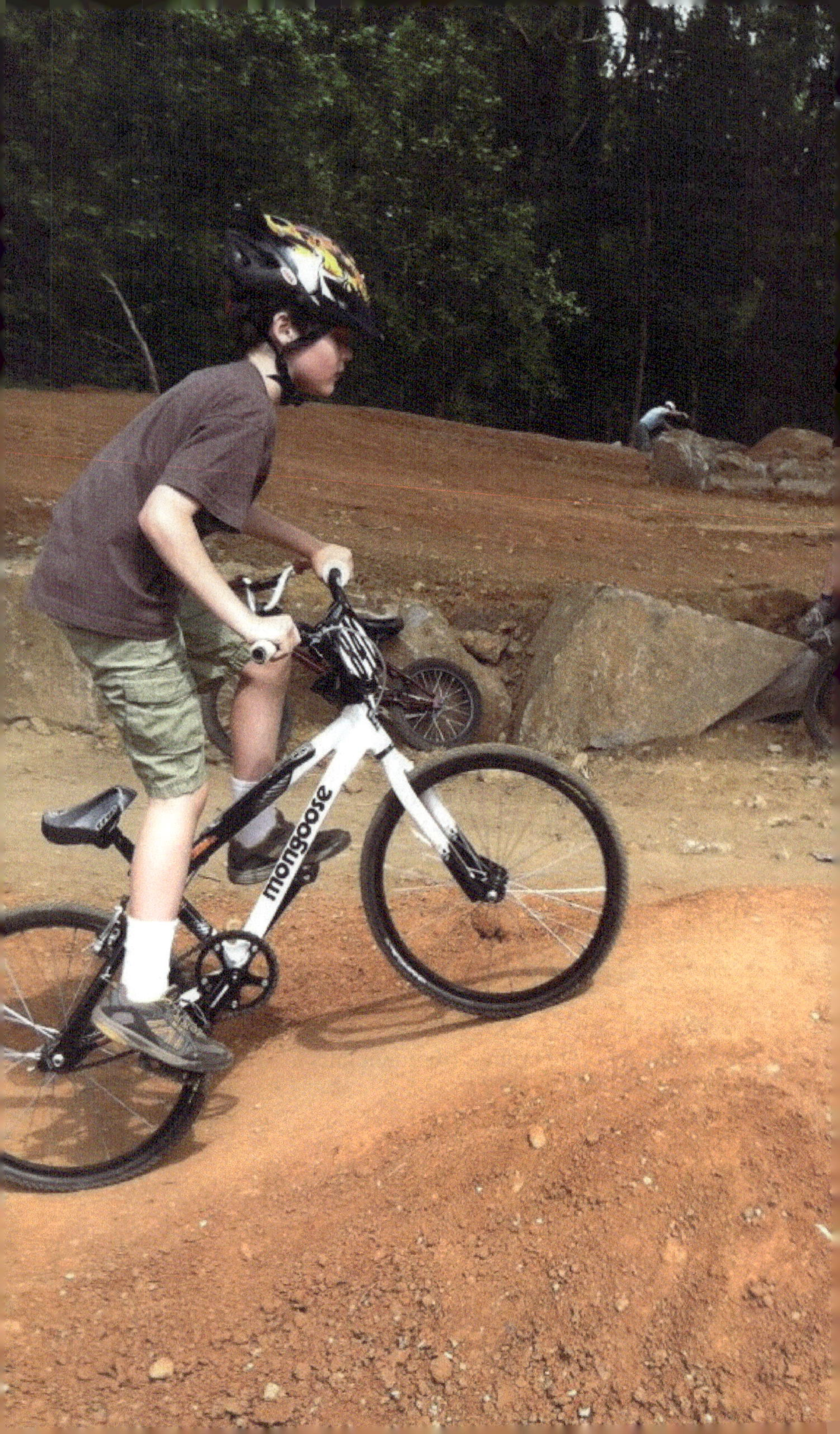
mongoose

- Dip each chicken breast in egg to coat.
- Dip each egg coated chicken breast with bread crumbs.
- Place chicken breasts in 9x13 baking dish. Pour 1 cup marinara over each chicken breast.
- Cover and bake 350 for 30 min.
- May sprinkle with Parmesan or low fat mozzarella cheese.

CHICKEN SPAGHETTI (VERSION 1)

1 package whole wheat spaghetti
1 can Rotel diced tomatoes
Cheese sauce (see recipe below)
2 yellow squash (optional - sneaky)
2 cups of rotisserie chicken or 2-3 chicken breasts

- Cook spaghetti according to directions. Drain and return to pot.
- If using chicken breasts, bake 350 for 30 minutes. Cut into bite size pieces.
- If sneaking in squash, cube and boil until tender.
- Make cheese sauce. Puree cooked squash with ½ cup or so sauce in food processor/blender.
- Pour Rotel, cheese sauce and chicken into pot with spaghetti.
- Mix together and pour in casserole dish.
- Bake 350 for 20-25 minutes.

Cheese sauce:
3 cups low sodium, fat-free chicken broth
4 TBSP light butter
½ cup whole wheat flour
2 cups low fat shredded cheddar
1 cup skim milk

- Melt butter in medium saucepan and add flour.
- Add chicken broth and milk. Heat on medium heat stirring constantly until thickens.
- Add shredded cheddar until melted.

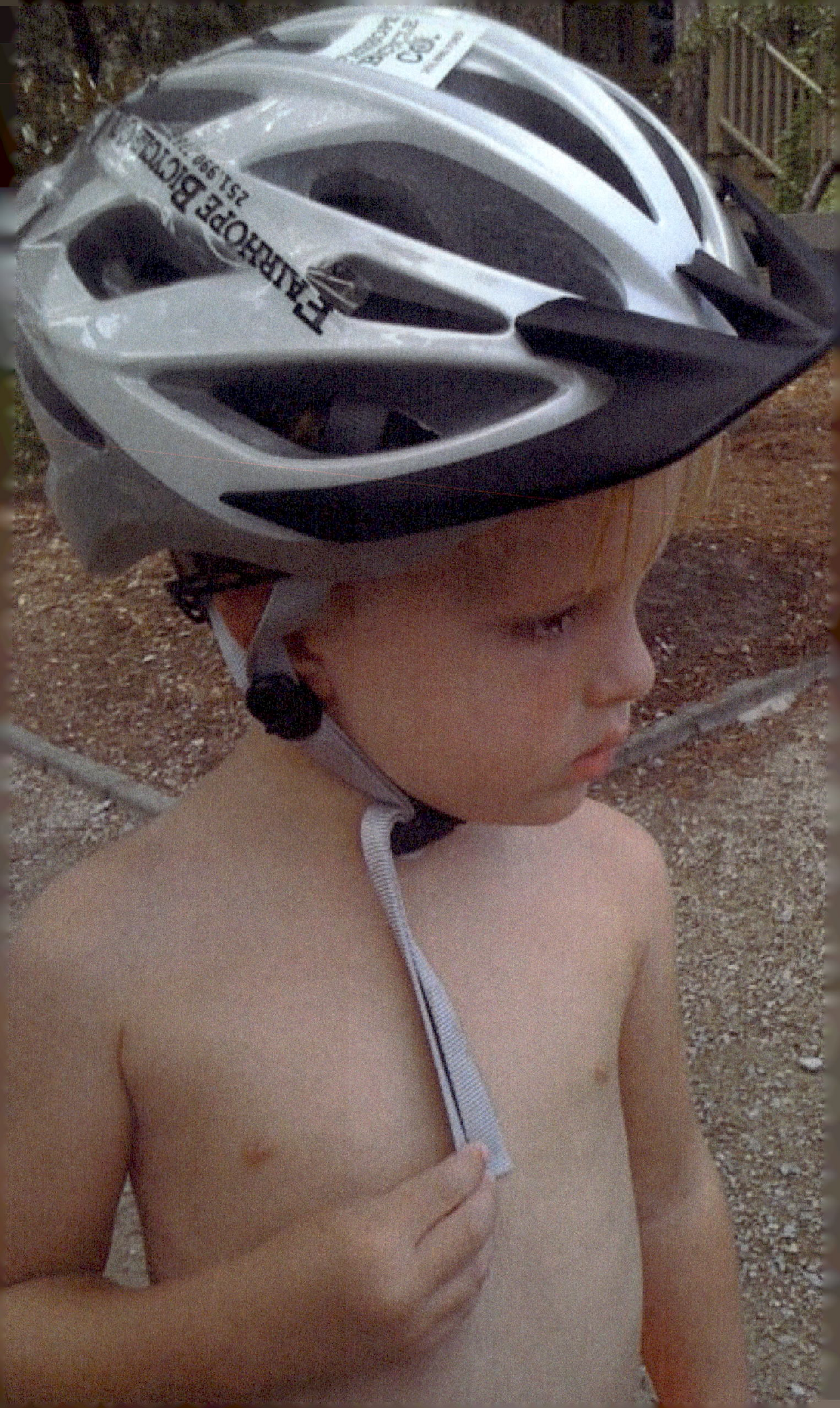
FAIRHOPE

CHICKEN SPAGHETTI (VERSION 2)

8oz package of whole wheat spaghetti
2 cans Campbell's Healthy Request cream of chicken soup
1 cup nonfat milk
2 cups low fat shredded cheddar cheese
2 cups chicken (rotisserie is easy)
1 TBSP light salted butter
½ cup finely chopped celery (optional)
½ cup finely chopped onion (optional)
½ cup sliced mushrooms (optional)
½ cup finely chopped red bell pepper (optional)

- Cook noodles according to directions. Drain. Return to pot.
- While noodles are cooking, sautee vegetables in butter (if using) in large skillet.
- Mix soup and milk together and add to skillet.
- Add 1 cup low fat shredded cheddar to skillet mixture. Pour skillet mixture over spaghetti in pot.
- Blend together. Pour in casserole dish. Bake 350 for 25min. Top with remaining cup of shredded cheddar and allow melt.

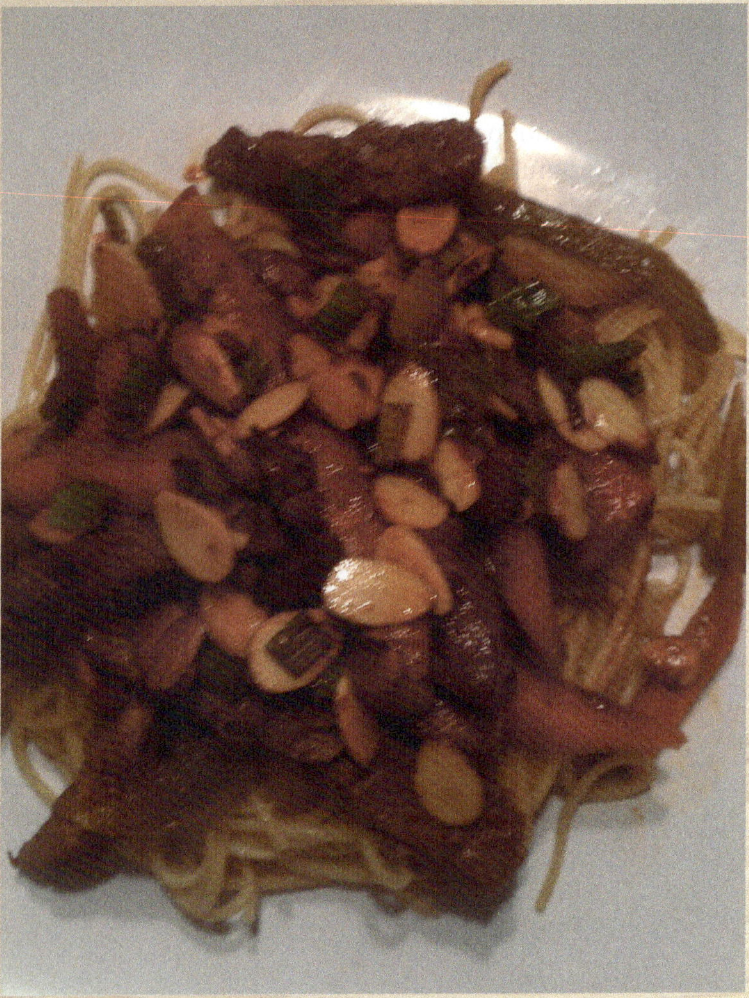

DADDY'S ASIAN BEEF & RICE

Makes 4 servings
Serving size: 1 cup of beef mixture over ½ cup rice

16 oz Sirloin steak (4 4oz sirloin steaks)
1 bell pepper (any color) – thinly sliced (about 1/8 inch wide)
1 stalk celery chopped
1 small onion thinly sliced (about 1/8 inch wide)
1 cup brown rice, whole wheat noodles or quinoa (allow 25 min)

Brown rice, quinoa or whole wheat noodles:
- Cook according to package directions. Allow 25 minutes for quinoa.

Sauce (start with these measurements and adjust to your liking):
- 1 can fat-free beef broth
- 1 TBSP tomato paste
- 2 tsp soy sauce
- 1 tsp fresh ginger – grated
- Pinch of sugar substitute
- Put all ingredients in small saucepan. Heat through.
  (if like spicy, may add Sirachi or Tiger sauce)

Steak:
- In large skillet, sear steaks on both sides (approximately 3 minutes per side on medium-high heat).
- Set steaks to the side and cook vegetables and sauce.
- Slice steaks into strips – between ½ to ¼ thickness. (Meat may be slightly undercooked but will finish cooking when combined in skillet with veggies and sauce.)

Vegetables:
- Coat another large skillet with nonstick cooking spray
- Saute vegetables until tender

Place meat, vegetables, and sauce in large skillet. Gently blend. Serve over rice or noodles. We sprinkle with slivered almonds.

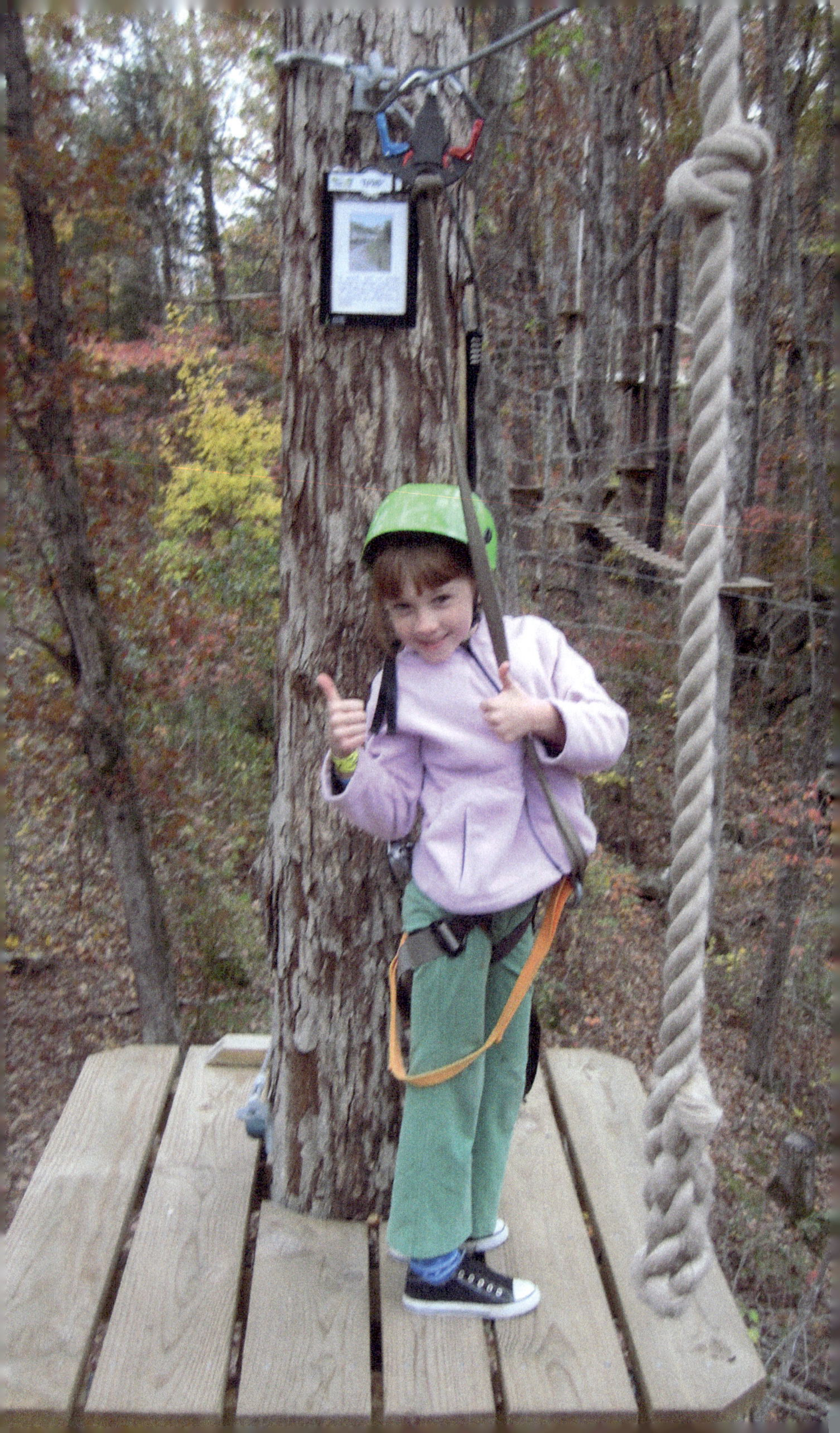

DADDY'S MARINARA

28oz can diced tomatoes
1 bell pepper (I use red to "blend in") cut in large chunks
2 large carrots cut in large chunks
1 large zucchini peeled and cut into large chunks
1 TBSP oregano
1 tsp onion powder
½ TBSP garlic powder
½ TBSP salt
1 tsp pepper
1 tsp sugar
1 small can tomato sauce
May add mushrooms or any additional vegetables of your choice

- Boil carrots and bell pepper until tender.
- Put tomato sauce, tomatoes, and boiled vegetables in food processor/blender until smooth.
- *I have to do the above steps since my children will not eat "chunky" tomato sauce. If yours don't have a problem with it, then just dice the veggies and throw in a large pot with tomatoes.
- Pour all vegetables in a pot.
- Add all seasonings.
- Heat on medium heat until heated through.
- Feel free to add more seasonings according to your taste.

FETTUCCINE ALFREDO
Makes 4-6 servings

8oz whole wheat fettuccine noodles
3 TBSP whole wheat flour
2 TBSP light butter
1.5 cups skim milk
½ cup grated Parmesan cheese
Salt and pepper to taste

- Cook noodles according to directions. Drain and return to pot.
- In medium saucepan, melt butter with flour over medium heat, whisking constantly.

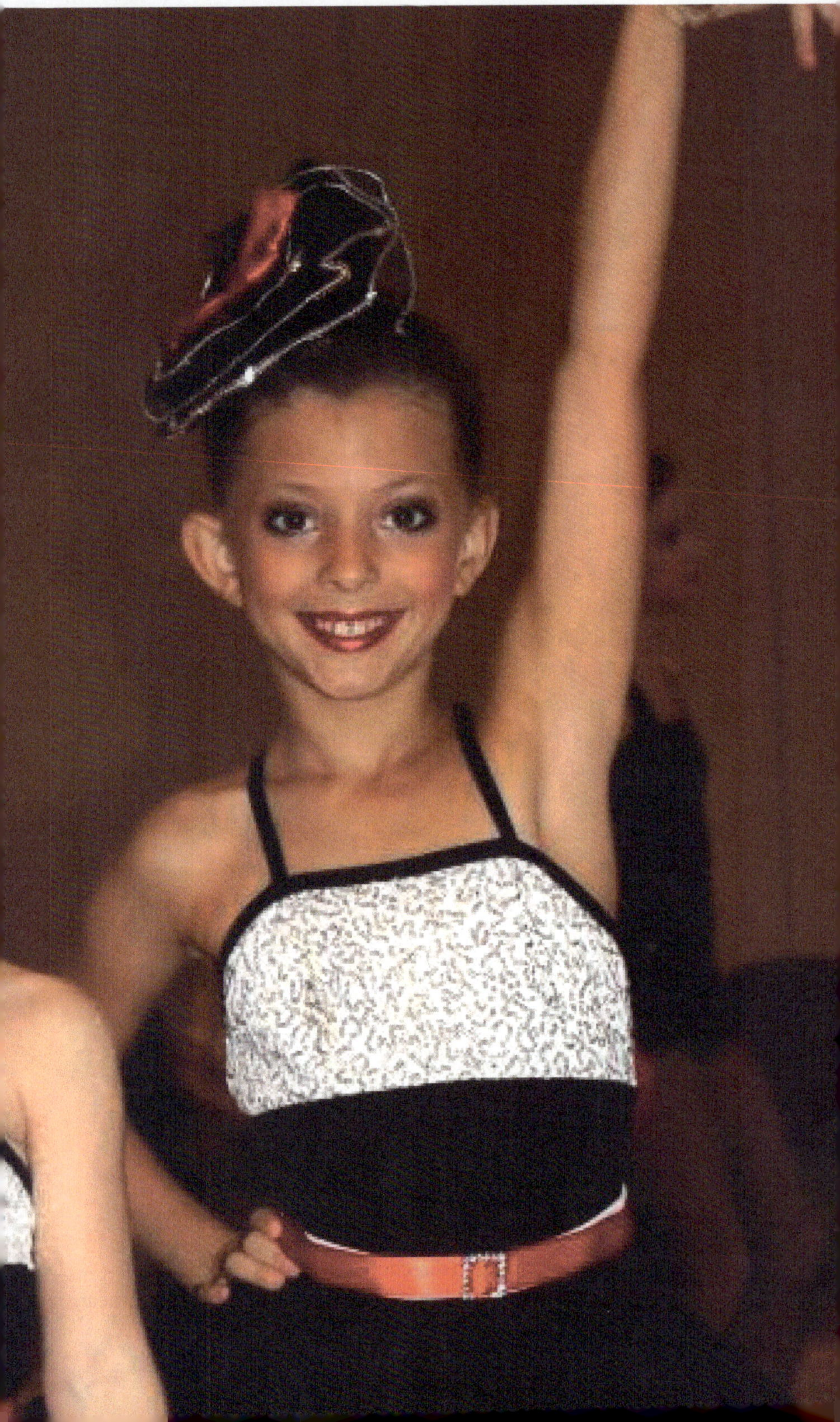

- Add milk. Whisk constantly until milk mixture thickens. May need to increase heat to thicken faster.
- Add cheese and continue to stir until melted.
- Salt and pepper to taste.
- Pour sauce over noodles and toss until coated.
- Add a cup of baked chicken or sautéed shrimp if you like.

GRILLED CAULIFLOWER

My 10 yr old insisted I put this recipe in here. She loves it! She says it tastes like French fries! Yay!

1 head cauliflower with florets removed from stem
Extra virgin olive oil
Garlic Salt

- Coat cauliflower with olive oil.
- Coat with garlic salt.
- Grill until starts to brown.

ISLAND CHICKEN

Serving: 1 completed chicken breast with ½ cup rice/quinoa (+ vegetables/salad)

4 chicken breasts
1 jar salsa
1 can sliced black olives
Artichoke hearts peeled into "leaves"
Fat-free or low fat feta cheese
1 cup uncooked brown rice or quinoa (allow 25 minutes for cooking)

- Cook chicken breasts 350 for 30-35 minutes.
- While chicken is baking, boil brown rice (or quinoa) according to directions.
- Top with ½ cup salsa.
- Top with TBSP sliced olives.
- Top with about ¼ cup artichokes leaves.
- Sprinkle with feta.

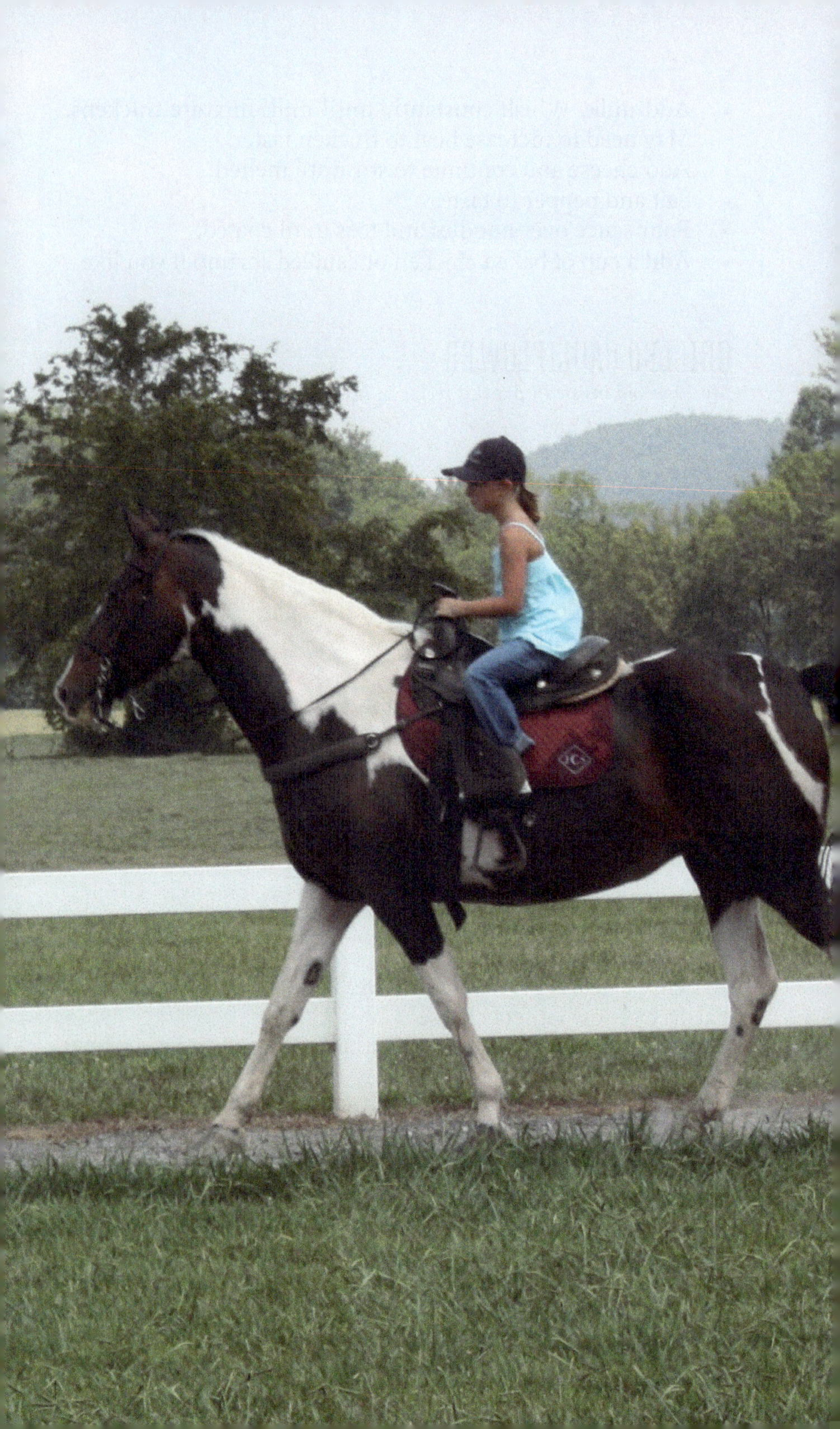

LASAGNA

Serving size: 2"x4" piece

"Daddy's Marinara Sauce" (see pg. 87)
1 box whole wheat lasagna noodles
15oz low fat ricotta cheese
1 cup low fat shredded mozarella cheese
1 bag fresh spinach (optional)
Low fat shredded mozzarella cheese
*1 lb ground breast of turkey (optional)

- Make marinara sauce.
- Boil lasagna noodles according to directions. Drain.
- While noodles are cooking, brown turkey if using. Drain and season with salt and pepper.
- Steam or sauté spinach if using.
- Add meat to marinara if using meat.
- Cover bottom of 9x12 dish with thin layer of marinara sauce.
- Layer noodles → cheese → spinach (if using) → sauce. Repeat. Top layer should be sauce.
- Bake 350 for 30 min.
- When 5 minutes remains on timer, sprinkle top with shredded mozzarella.

LASAGNA II

Same recipe as above except substitute 1 eggplant for whole wheat lasagna noodles. Peel eggplant and cut into long, thin slices using carrot peeler. Do not need to boil eggplant. Layer raw and follow layers as above.

MAC'N'CHEESE

8oz whole wheat elbow macaroni (I usually do 12 oz for leftovers)
16oz low fat cottage cheese (1%)
1-2 cups cauliflower or squash (optional – sneaky)
8oz fat-free or low-fat sour cream
2 egg whites
2 cups low fat shredded cheddar
Splash of skim milk
Salt and pepper to taste

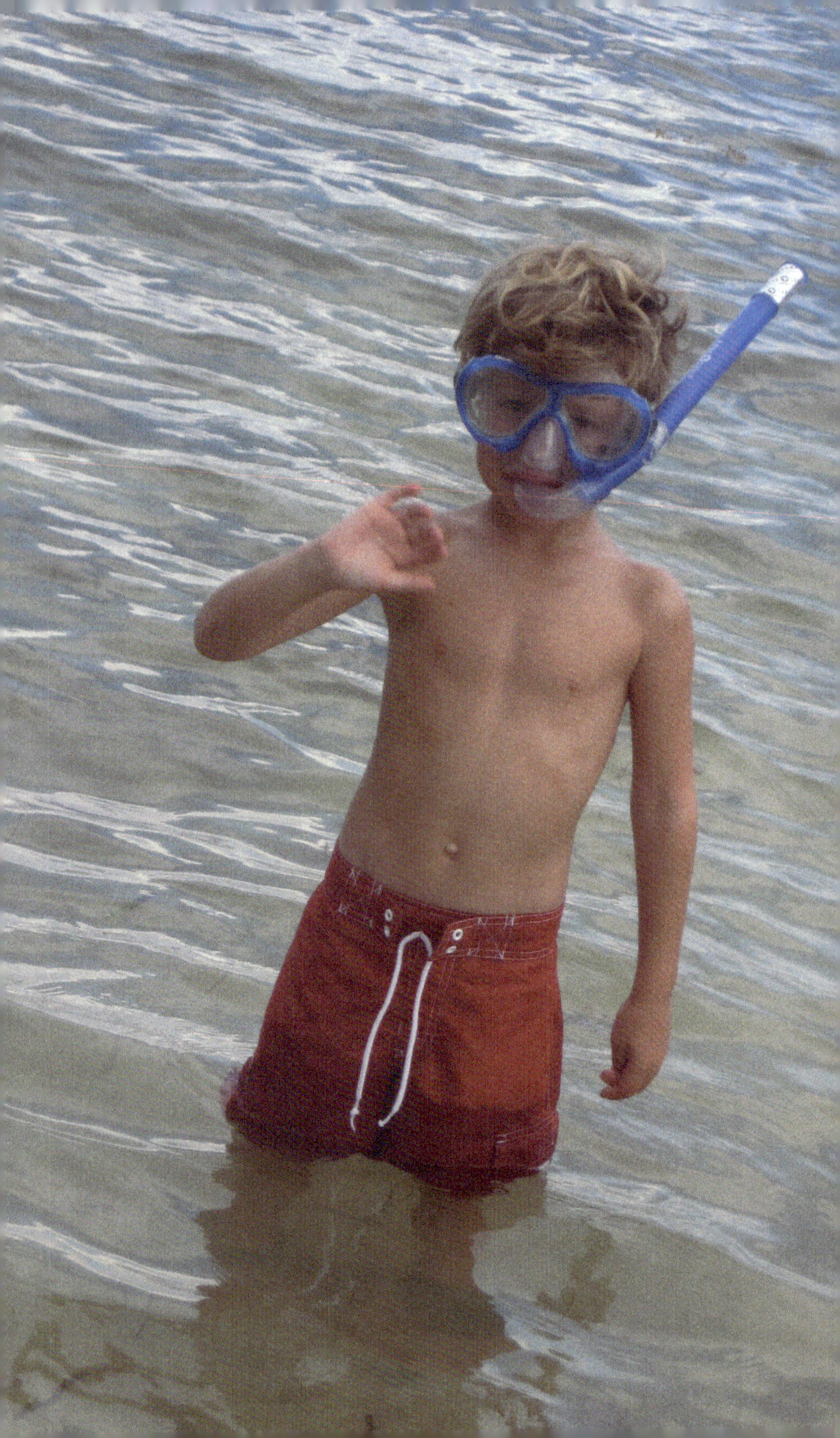

- Cook elbow macaroni according to directions.
- Boil cauliflower or squash until tender; drain.
- Puree cauliflower or squash with sour cream.
- Mix sour cream (or sour cream/veggie mixture), cottage cheese, egg whites, and 1.5 cups cheddar in large bowl.
- Add macaroni and stir until well blended.
- Bake 350 for 30-40 minutes.
- Top with remaining 1/2 cup cheddar and allow to melt.

MANICOTTI OR STUFFED PASTA SHELLS
Makes 14 pieces

Ingredients for "Daddy's" marinara (see pg. 87)
Whole wheat manicotti or large pasta shells
1 head cauliflower
15 oz low fat ricotta cheese
2 cups low fat shredded mozzarella
2 cups low fat or fat free cottage cheese
1-2 cups cooked spinach (optional)
1 tsp nutmeg (optional)
Salt and pepper to taste

- Make "Daddy's" Marinara
- Boil manicotti or shells according to directions. Drain. Set aside.
- Cut cauliflower into large florets. Boil until VERY tender. Drain. Blend until smooth.
- Combine all cheeses in large bowl. Stir in pureed cauliflower.
- Add spinach and nutmeg if using.
- Salt and pepper cheese filling to taste.
- Stuff manicotti or pasta shells.
- Cover with marinara.
- Cover dish with foil and bake 350 for 25 minutes.

MASHED POTATOES

1 large head of cauliflower
1 potato cut in chunks
1 small onion cut in chunks
6 cups chicken broth
2 TBSP light butter

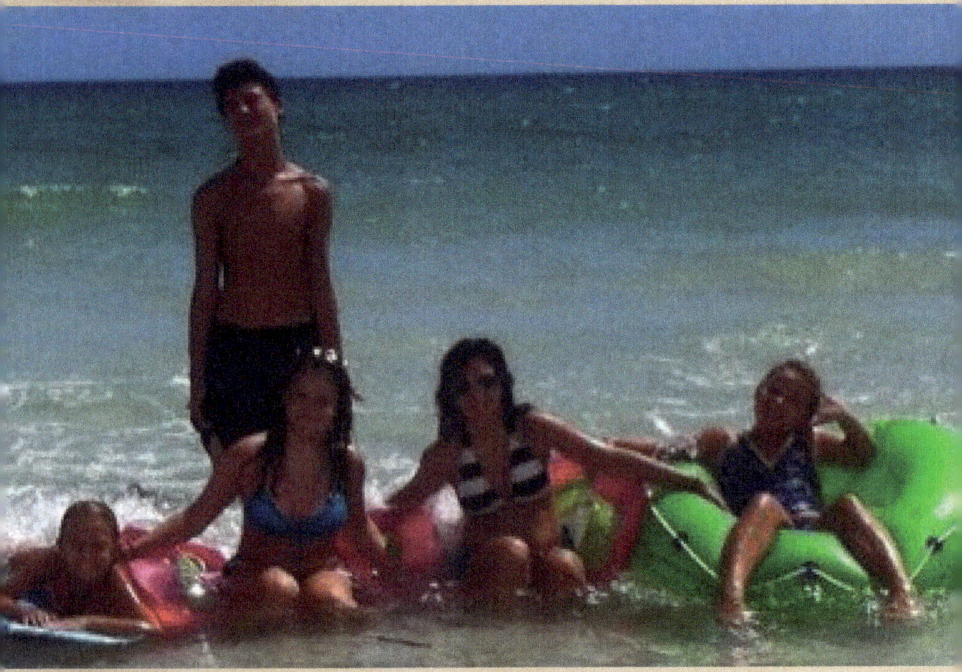

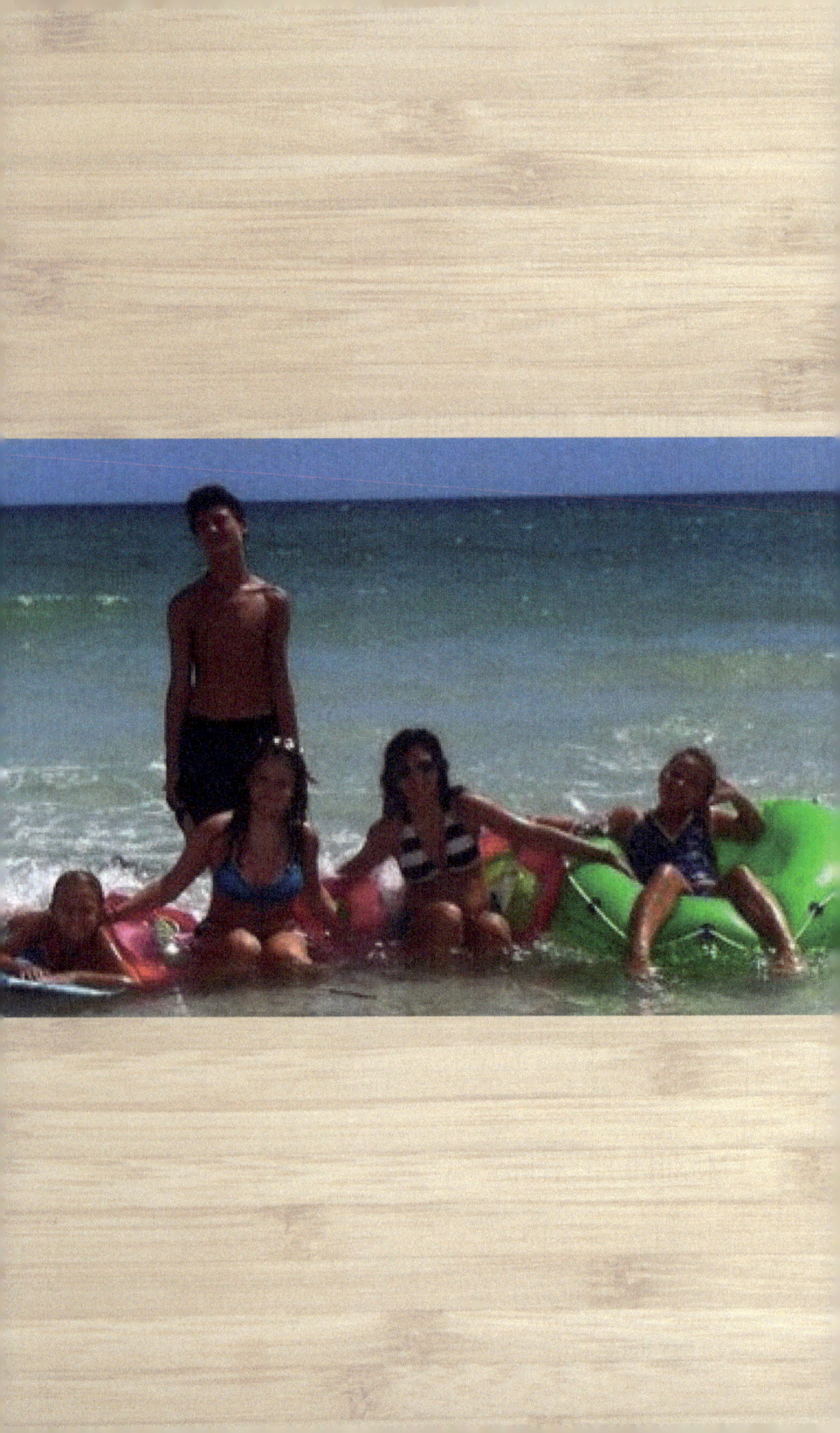

Splash of fat free milk (optional to texture preference)
Salt and pepper to taste

- Boil cauliflower, cubed potato, and onion in broth. Drain saving ¼ cup broth. Set aside.
- Place cauliflower, onion, and potato in blender without broth. Blend until just smooth.
- Add reserved ¼ cup broth and pulse a few times.
- Pour in large serving dish/bowl.
- Add butter.
- Add splash of fat free milk if needed for texture.
- Add salt and pepper to taste.

MEATLOAF
Yields 12 slices

1 cup whole wheat breadcrumbs (put whole wheat bread slices into food processor/blender)
4 oz Carnation low fat condensed milk OR skim milk
½ cup ketchup
1 tsp mustard
1 lb ground breast of turkey (raw)
½ cup chopped onion
1/3 cup finely chopped bell pepper (color your choice)
1 TBSP Worcestershire sauce
1 TBSP brown sugar substitute
1 tsp dried basil
¾ tsp salt
¼ tsp ground black pepper
3 large egg whites
Cooking spray

- Preheat oven to 350.
- Place breadcrumbs and milk in bowl and soak about 5 minutes.
- Add 2 TBSP of ketchup and remaining ingredients. Mix with hands until well blended.
- Coat 9x5 loaf pan with cooking spray.
- Shape meat mixture into loaf pan.
- Coat meatloaf with ketchup sauce. (See recipe below.)
- Bake 350 for 1 hour. Let stand 10 minutes.

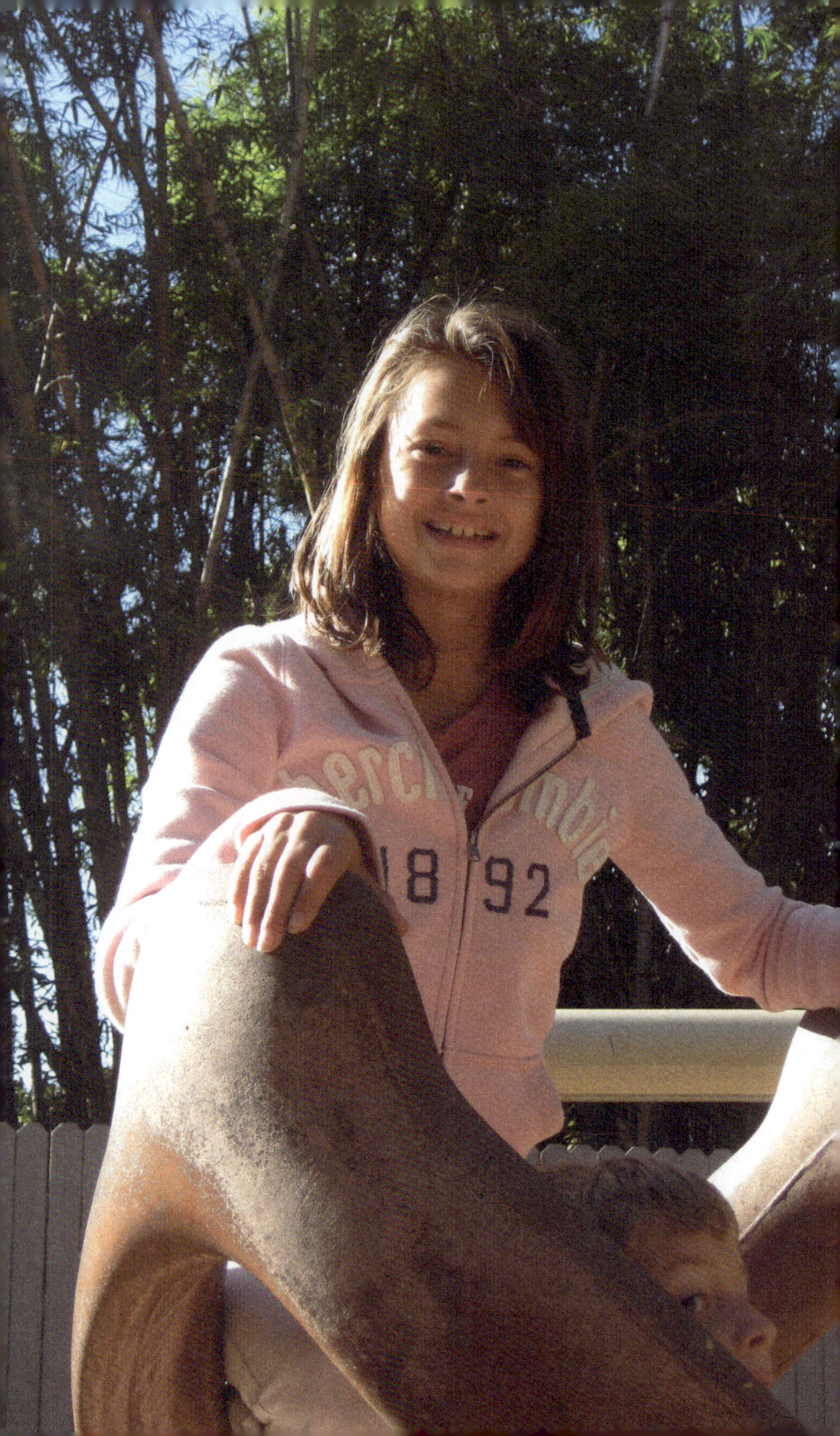
18 92

Sauce:
Remaining ketchup
2 TBSP brown sugar substitute
1 TBSP yellow mustard

MEXICAN CORN

Fresh corn on the cob – boiled or grilled
TBSP nonfat or low fat sour cream
TBSP Parmesan Cheese
Sea Salt and Pepper to taste

- Thinly smear sour cream on cob until fully coated.
- Sprinkle parmesan cheese on cob until lightly coated.
- Add small amount sea salt and pepper to taste.
- *May add tobasco sauce or chili powder if you like spicy.

MEXICAN RICE

Makes 4 servings

1 cup uncooked brown rice or quinoa (allow 25 minutes)
2 cups low sodium fat-free chicken broth
1 TBSP light butter
1 packet taco seasoning
1 small can corn
½ can green chiles
¼ cup diced onion
¼ cup red bell pepper

- Cook rice or quinoa according to directions in chicken broth.
- While rice is cooking, coat small skillet with cooking spray and sauté onion and pepper until onion is transparent.
- Drain rice or quinoa and return to pot. Stir in 1 TBSP light butter, taco seasoning to taste, chiles, corn, onion and bell pepper.

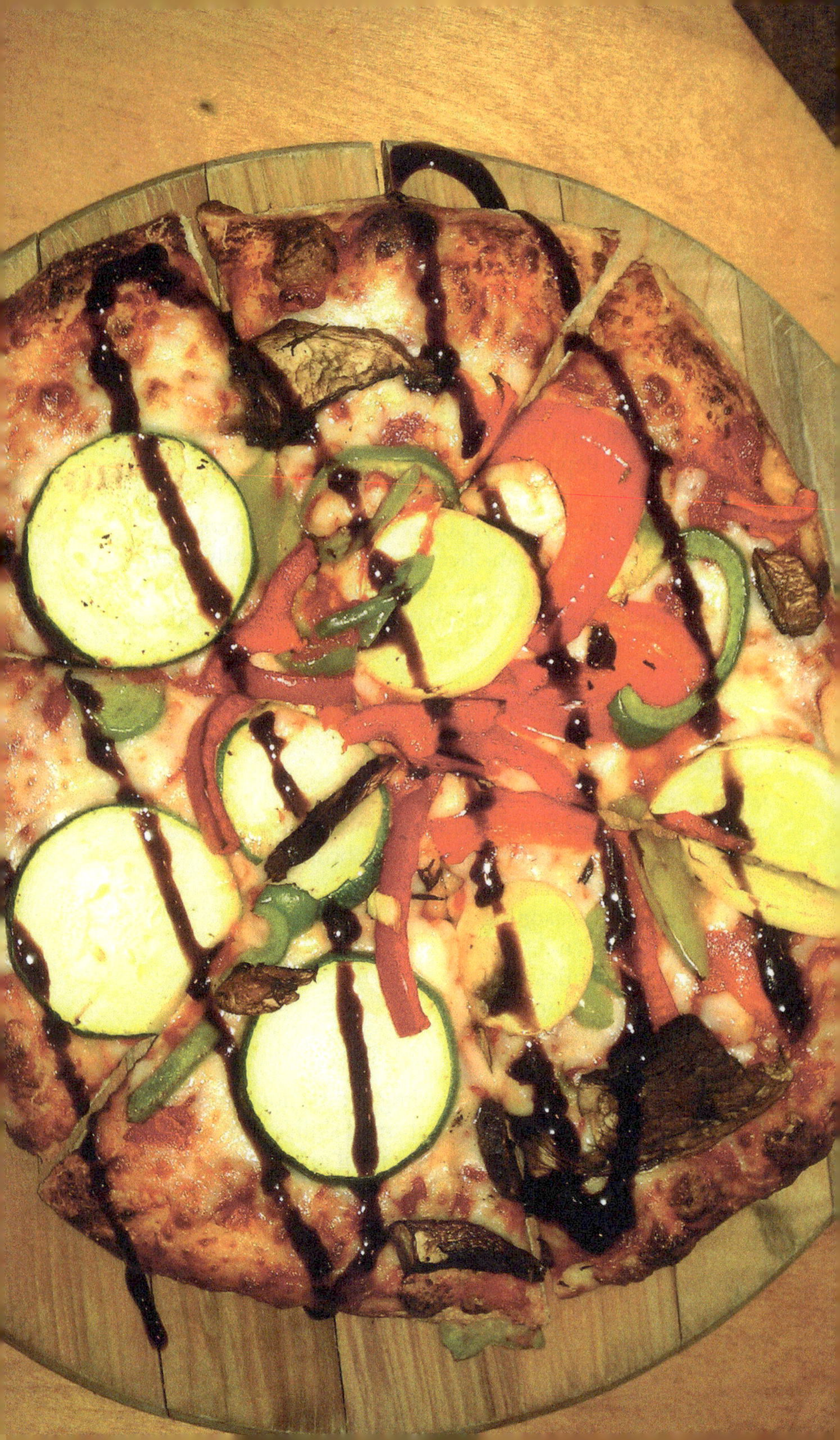

MUSHROOM RICE
Makes 4 servings

1 cup uncooked brown rice or quinoa (allow 25 minutes)
2 cups fat free, low sodium chicken broth
1 TBSP light butter
½ can Campbell's healthy request cream of mushroom
Splash of skim milk
1/2-1 cup fresh mushrooms diced (optional)
1 cup diced fresh mushrooms, sauteed (optional)

- Cook rice in broth according to directions. Drain and return to pot.
- While rice is cooking, sautee diced mushrooms and stir into soup.
- Add 1 TBSP light butter and stir in cream of mushroom soup.
- Add splashes of milk until achieve desired texture.

PIZZA (SOME OF OUR FAVORITES)
Serving size: 2 slices (1 slice = 1/8 of pizza)

Crust	Sauce	Topping	Cheese
Bobilio's whole wheat crust	1 cup BBQ	2 cups baked or rotisserie chicken Red onion (optional)	1 cup low fat shredded mozarella
Bobilio's whole wheat crust	Daddy's Marinara (pg. 87)	20-24 turkey pepperoni	1 cup low fat shredded mozarella
Bobilio's whole wheat crust	Alfredo sauce (pg. 87)	20-24 sauteed shrimp + any vegetables	1 cup low fat shredded mozarella
Bobilio's whole wheat crust	Daddy's Marinara (pg. 87)	all the vegetables you want!	1 cup low fat shredded mozarella

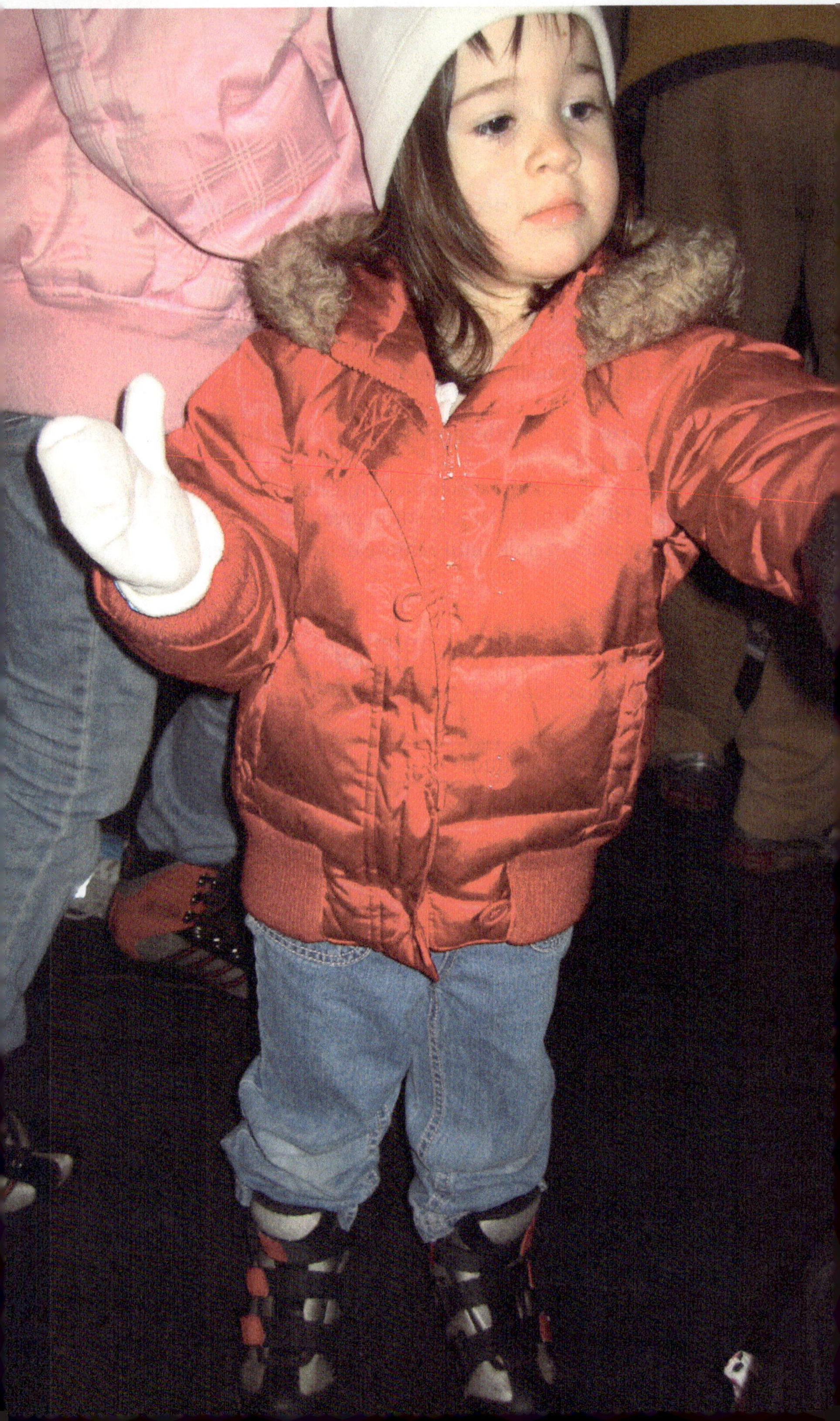

PIZZA BURGERS

Whole Wheat hamburger buns
1lb ground breast of turkey
Daddy's marinara (see pg. 87)
Low fat mozzarella

- In large skillet, brown turkey. Drain if needed. Return to skillet.
- Add marinara to turkey. Stir until well blended.
- Place ¼ cup mixture on each bun and top with mozzarella.

PORK TENDERLOIN AND SWEET COUSCOUS
Kaitlin Moore, 9 years old

1/2 cup Apricot preserves (best are bought at the farmers market)
1 ½ cups reduced sodium fat-free chicken broth
½ tsp hot pepper flakes
1 (5.8) box plain couscous or quinoa
1 cup frozen peas, thawed (you can use edamame too)
1 large pork tenderloin
McCormick grill mates low-sodium Montreal chicken seasoning

- Rub tenderloin evenly with seasoning.
- Grill or broil pork for 20 minutes, turning occasionally, or until meat is cooked through and registers 145 on instant read thermometer. Cover and let rest 5 minutes before slicing.
- While pork cooks, place broth and hot pepper flakes in small saucepan; bring to a boil.
- Stir in couscous, peas and apricot preserves (about 5 TBS); cover and remove from heat. Let stand 5 minutes.

Optional: you can add chopped red onion to top of couscous.

RAINBOW RICE

1 cup uncooked brown rice or quinoa (allow 25 minutes to cook)
2 cups low sodium, fat-free chicken broth
1 TBSP light butter
12oz bag frozen vegetables
½ cup red bell pepper diced (optional)
¼ cup onion diced (optional)
Cooking spray

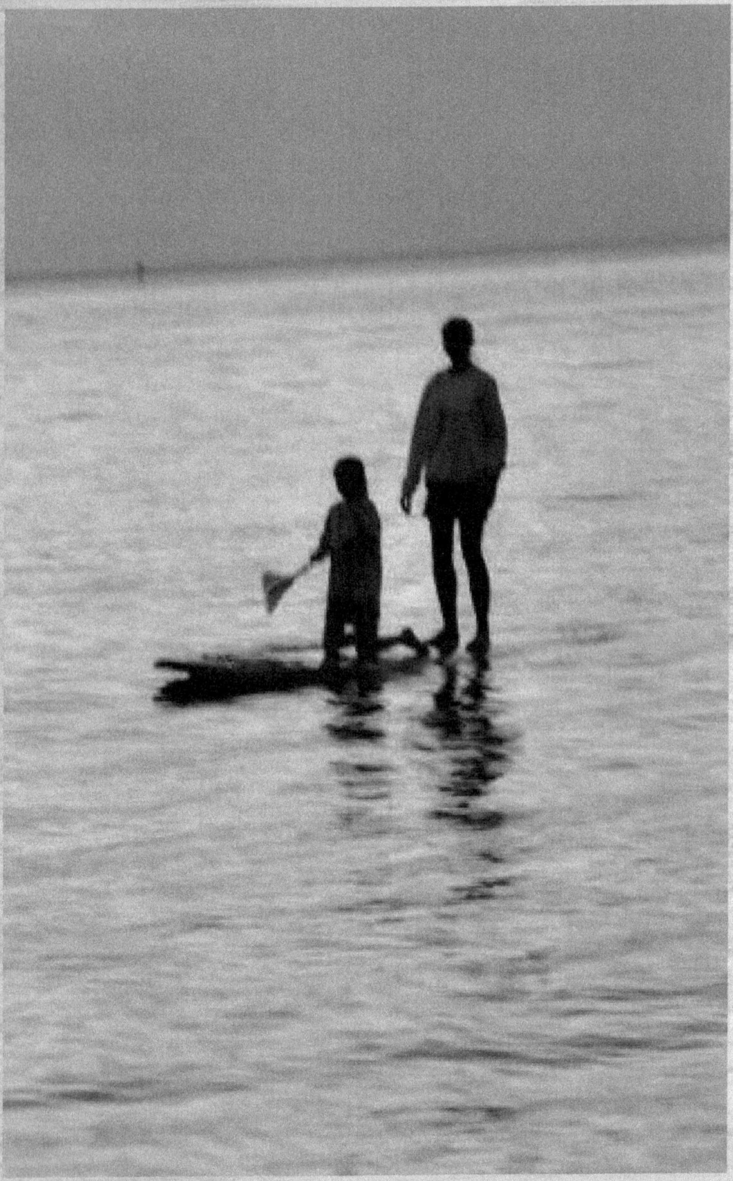

- Cook rice or quinoa in broth according to directions. Drain. Return to pot. Fluff and add 1 TBSP light salted butter.
- Coat small skillet with cooking spray. Saute bell pepper and onion until tender.
- Cook vegetables according to direction.
- Mix all together. Salt and Pepper to taste.

NOTE: My children like to add a touch of low sodium soy sauce.

RISOTTO

Makes 8 servings
From the kitchen of Mia 9, Rhodes 8, Morgan 8, and mom Carrie

2 cups quinoa (allow 25 minutes to cook)
4 cups low sodium, fat-free chicken broth
1 rotisserie chicken (or 3-4 cooked chicken breasts)
1 TBSP extra virgin olive oil
2 shallots minced
2 gloves garlic minced
3 stalks of celery finely chopped
1-1.5 TBSP light salted butter
1 cup reduced fat grated parmesan cheese
2-3 slices fresh reduced fat mozzarella cheese
*Cherry tomatoes – see note
*Fresh basil leaves – see note

- Cook quinoa in broth according to directions.
- While quinoa is cooking, sauté shallots, garlic, and celery in olive oil over medium heat. Cook until tender and set aside.
- Pull chicken meat from bones and skin into bite size pieces. Set aside.
- Once quinoa is done, allow to sit 5 minutes. Fluff with a fork. Stir in butter.
- Mix chicken, vegetables, and parmesan cheese into quinoa.
- Add cherry tomatoes and basil leaves if using.
- Pour into casserole dish.
- Cut mozzarella slices into quarters and scatter over top of dish.
- Bake 350 covered for 30 minutes.

*May add whatever vegetable you prefer if do not prefer cherry tomatoes.

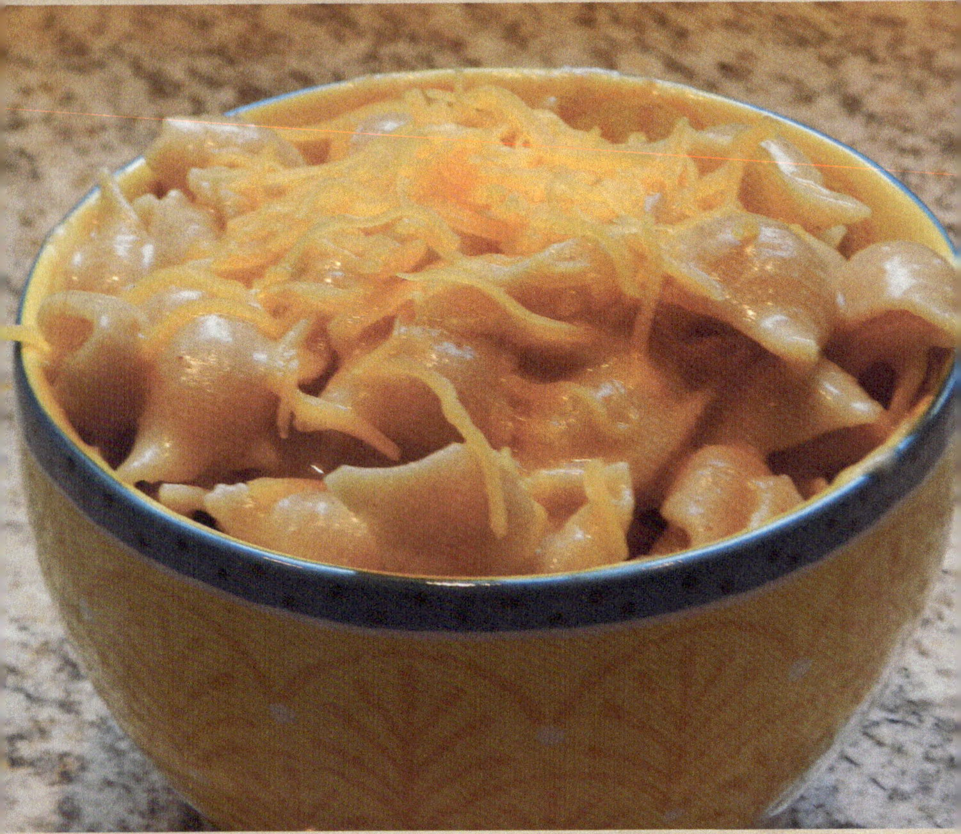

SHELLS'N'CHEESE

Makes 4-6 servings

1 box (8oz) whole wheat pasta shells
4 TBSP light butter
1/2 cup whole wheat flour
3 cups low sodium fat-free chicken broth
1 cup skim milk
2 cups reduced fat shredded cheddar
2 yellow squash (optional - sneaky)
Salt and pepper to taste

- Cook pasta shells according to directions. Drain. Return to pot.
- Boil squash until tender if using. Drain and set aside.
- Melt butter and flour in medium saucepan over medium heat. Stir with whisk until butter is melted.
- Stir in broth and milk. Increase heat to medium-high. Whisk constantly until sauce thickens. Usually takes 15-20 min.
- Add cheese until melted. Remove from heat.
- If using squash, puree in blender with about 1/2 cup of cheese sauce.
- Return to remaining cheese sauce. Stir well. Add salt and pepper to taste.
- Save ½ cup cheese sauce for next day leftovers (leftovers not that good with just adding milk to reheat).
- Pour remaining cheese sauce over pasta shells and stir until well coated.

SOUTHWEST CHICKEN

4 chicken breasts
1 packet fajita seasoning
½ cup water
2 cups salsa
4 oz low fat shredded cheddar
Low fat sour cream

- Mix fajita seasoning and water for marinade.
- Place chicken breasts in a gallon Ziploc bag. Pour marinade over chicken breasts. Place chicken breasts in refrigerator approximately one hour.
- Grill chicken breasts or bake 350 for 30 minutes.

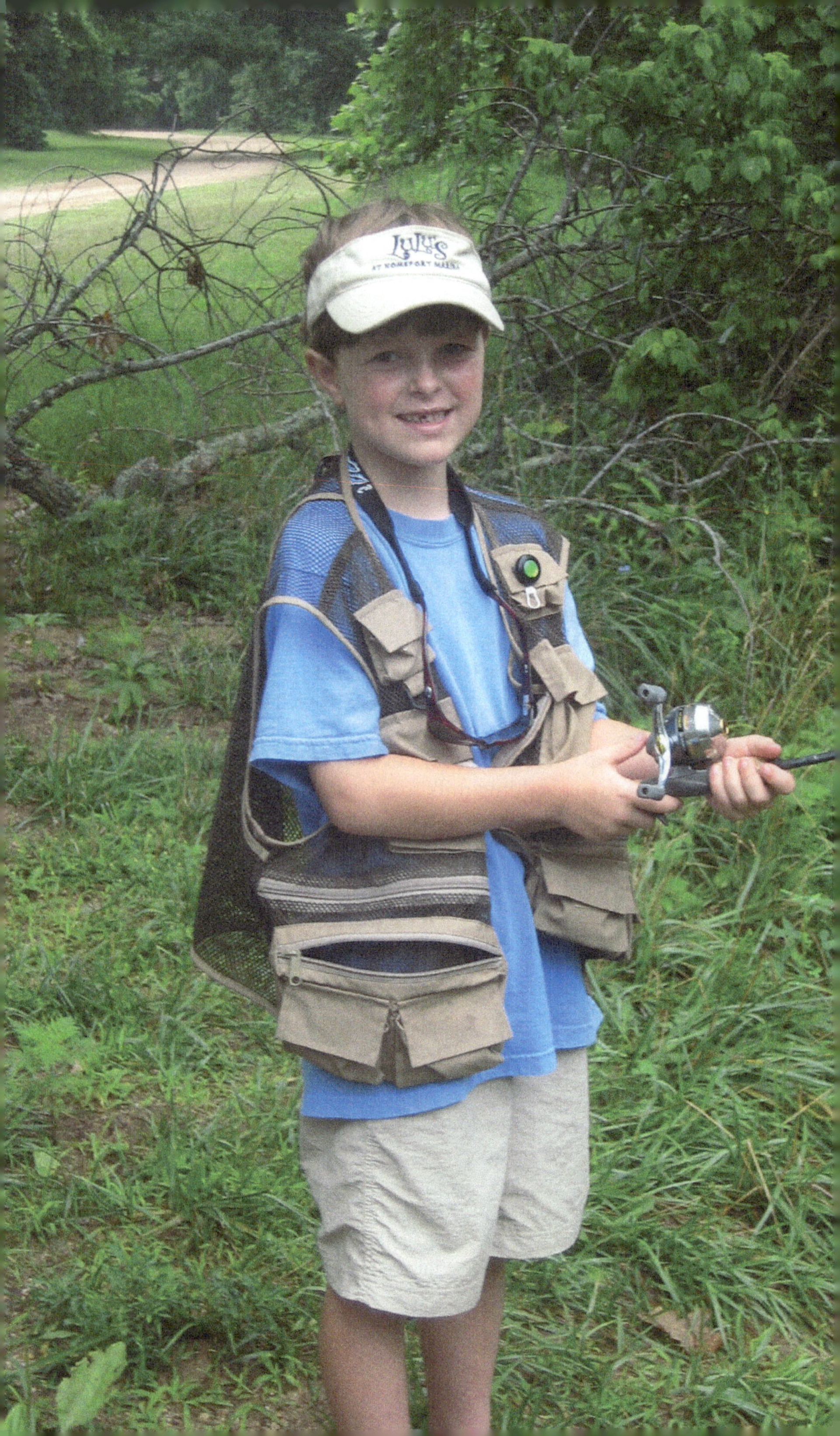

- Top each chicken breast with ½ cup salsa, 1oz shredded cheddar, and 1tsp sour cream.
- Serve over brown rice or Mexican rice (see recipe) + salad, corn salad and/or vegetables.

SWEET AND SOUR CHICKEN
Makes 4-6 servings
Adapted from www.eatingwell.com

2 cups brown rice or quinoa (allow 25 minutes to prepare)
¼ cup apple cider or rice vinegar
2 TBSP low sodium soy sauce
2 TBSP corn starch
2 TBSP apricot or peach preserves
½ tsp red pepper flakes (optional)
2 TBSP oil (canola, vegetable, coconut)
1 lb chicken cubed
4 cloves garlic, minced
2 tsp minced ginger
1 cup reduced sodium, fat free chicken broth
6 cups fresh vegetables (or frozen stir fry mix) such as carrots, broccoli, bell peppers, onions and peas.

- Cook rice or quinoa in water (or chicken broth) according to directions.
- While rice or quinoa is cooking, whisk together vinegar, soy sauce, cornstarch, fruit preserves, and red pepper flakes (optional) in small bowl. Set aside.
- Heat 1 TBSP oil in large skillet or wok on medium-high heat. Cook chicken until no longer pink and lightly browned. Remove and set aside.
- Add remaining TBSP of oil to skillet/wok. Cook garlic and ginger for about 30 seconds.
- Add broth. Stirring constantly, bring to a boil. Reduce to a simmer.
- Add all vegetables. Cover and cook until reach desired tenderness.
- Add chicken and sauce continuing to simmer until sauce thickens.
- Serve over rice or quinoa.

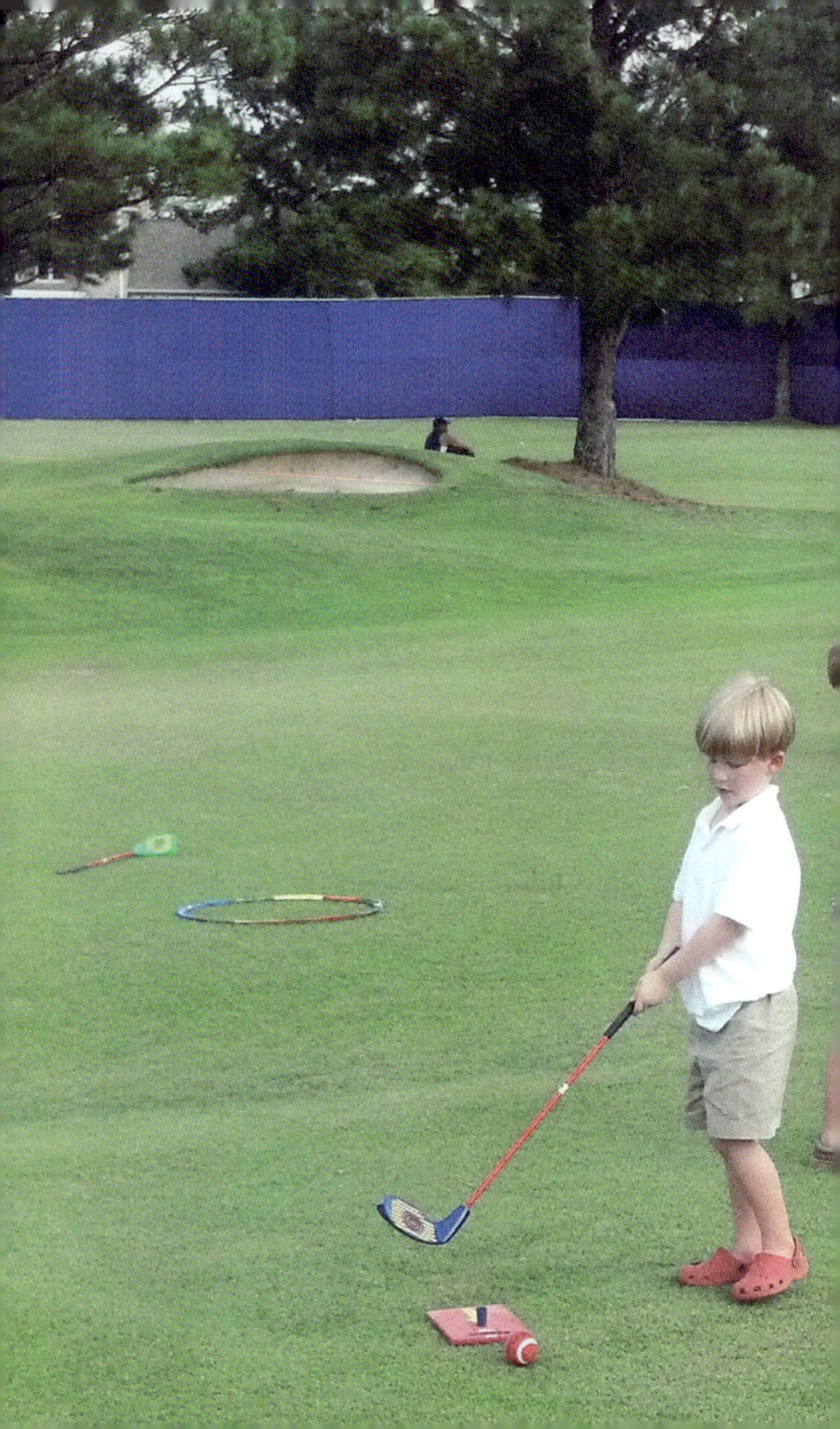

TACO CASSEROLE

Makes 6 servings
Adapted from Tastefully Simple

1 lb ground breast of turkey
1 packet taco seasoning (We only use half the packet.)
1 8oz jar salsa
6 whole wheat tortillas (We use Mission whole wheat carb balance tortillas.)
1 cup low fat shredded cheddar
*Optional – corn, sliced black olives and/or black beans

- Cut six tortillas into 1"-2" pieces. Set aside.
- In large skillet brown meat and drain.
- Add taco seasoning according to packet directions. Once taco seasoning and meat are done, stir in salsa.
- *Optional –may add sautéd vegetables of your choice and/or sliced black olives to mixture.
- Fold in tortilla pieces gently.
- Pour in 9x9 or 9x12 casserole dish. Cover and bake 350 20-25 minutes. When five minutes remains in cooking time, sprinkle top shredded cheddar and continue to bake until melted.

TACO POCKETS

	Protein Filler	Condiment Filler
Whole Wheat Pita Pocket +	Grilled/baked chicken pieces, Rotisserie chicken pieces, Grilled or sautéed shrimp, Ground breast of turkey, Black beans *season protein with taco seasoning if desired	Chopped lettuce, tomato, any vegetables of choice, Low fat sour cream, Fat-free ranch dressing, Fat-free catalina dressing, Low fat shredded cheddar

Choice of protein(s) + Choice of condiments + stuff in whole wheat pita half = taco pouches

5

SANDWICHES

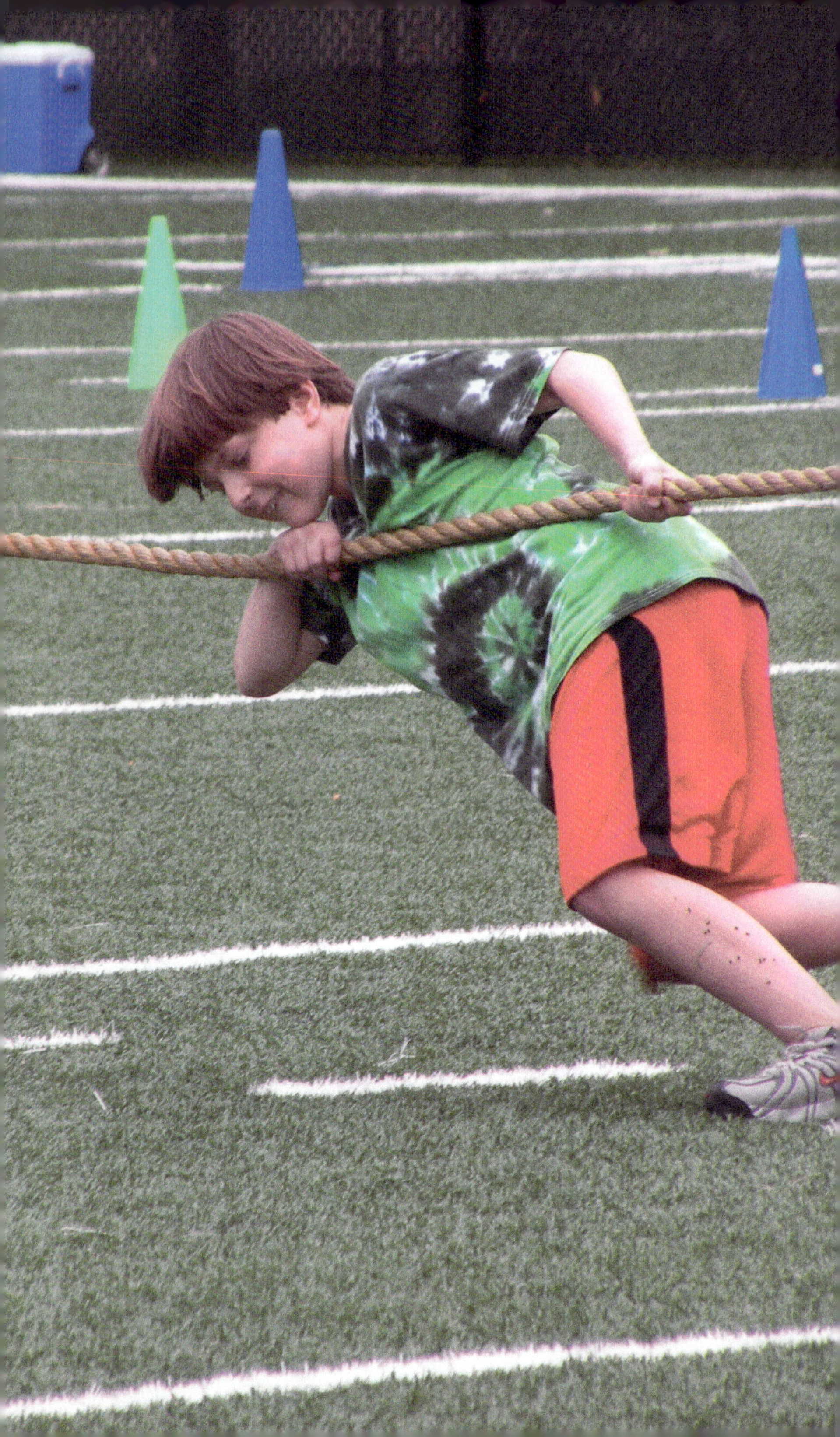

BUILD YOUR OWN

Bread	Meat	Fillers	Condiments 1-2 TBSP
Whole wheat bread, whole wheat tortilla, whole wheat pita, whole wheat bagel thin	2-3 slices counter deli meat or portion size of packaged deli meat	All the veggies you want OR Apple slices, pear slices, banana slices	Reduced fat cream cheese any flavor, Low fat shredded cheese or feta, fat free hummus, fat free salad dressing, natural peanut butter of PB2 Crunch

CHEESY RANCH ROLL-UPS

1 packet dry Ranch dressing mix
8oz tub of fat free or reduced fat cream cheese
1 pack whole wheat carb balance tortillas (We buy Mission.)
Low sodium deli turkey (We get Boar's Head.)

- Mix ¼ to ½ Ranch packet in tub of cream cheese (according to your taste).
- Spread cream cheese over tortilla.
- Top with turkey.
- Roll up and slice into ½ inch pieces.

*You can add any vegetables you like in the roll up.
*I keep a tub of the "herbed" cream cheese in my fridge at all times.

Alternative - use plain cream cheese instead of herb. Add granny smith or red apples slices on top of turkey.

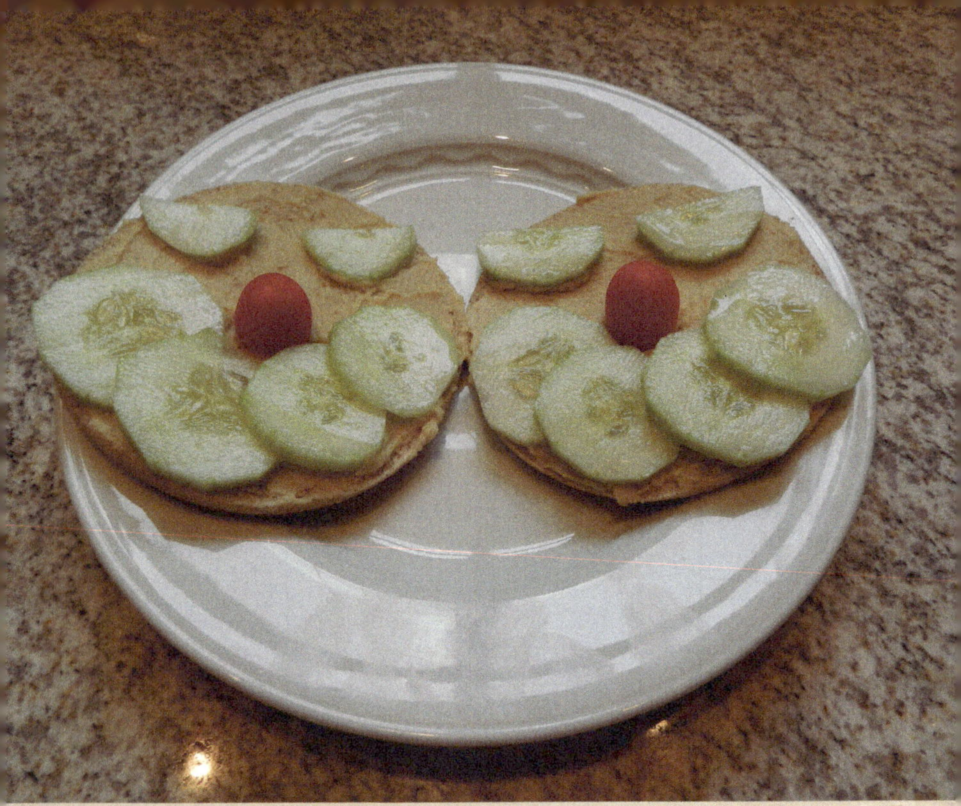

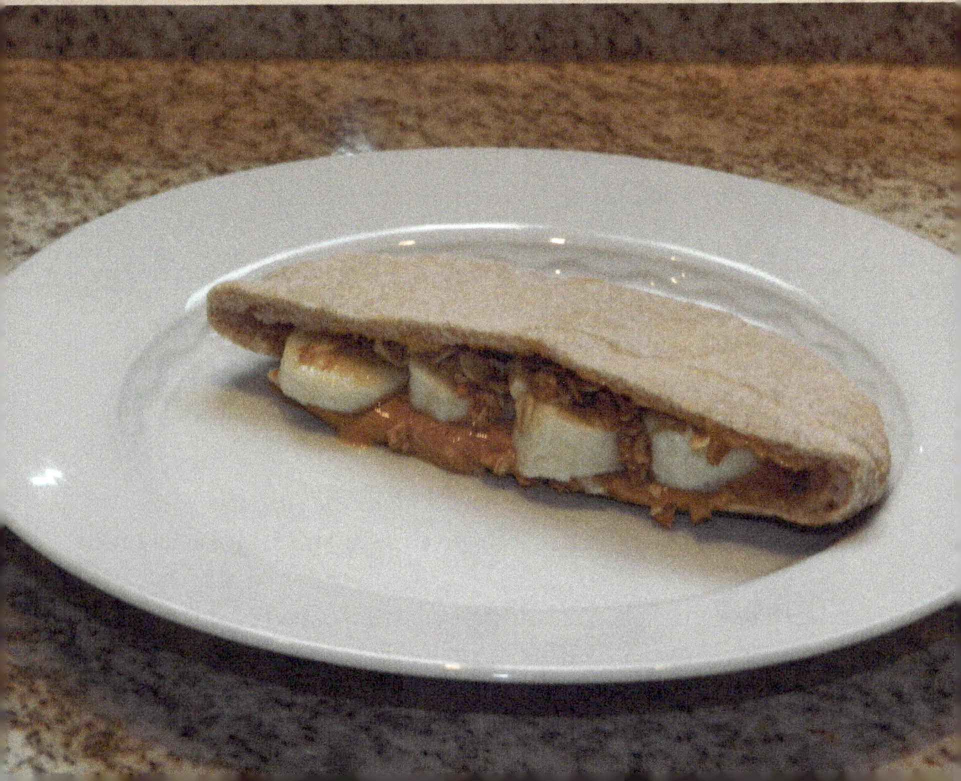

HAPPY HUMMUS

1 whole wheat bagel thin
1 container your favorite flavor of fat free hummus
1 cucumber peeled and sliced
1 cherry tomato

- Spread 1 TBSP hummus on bagel halves.
- Place cucumber slices on top off hummus to look like two eyes and a big smile.
- Place cherry tomato in hole of bagel for a "nose."
- You can eat halves separately or make eat like a sandwich.

STUFFED PEANUT BUTTER POUCH

1 whole wheat pita pocket
2 TBSP PB2 Crunch or natural peanut butter (no hydrogenated oils)
½ banana sliced
TBSP granola
Drizzle of honey or agave nectar (about 1 tsp)

- Spread PB2 Crunch or natural peanut butter inside one half of whole wheat pita.
- Pile in remaining ingredients.

TOMATO & MOZARELLA

1 whole wheat English muffin or whole wheat bagel thin - toasted
2 TBSP sun dried tomato spread
1 slice low fat fresh mozzarella (about ¼ inch)

- Spread 1 TBSP sun dried tomato spread on both sides of English muffin or bagel thin.

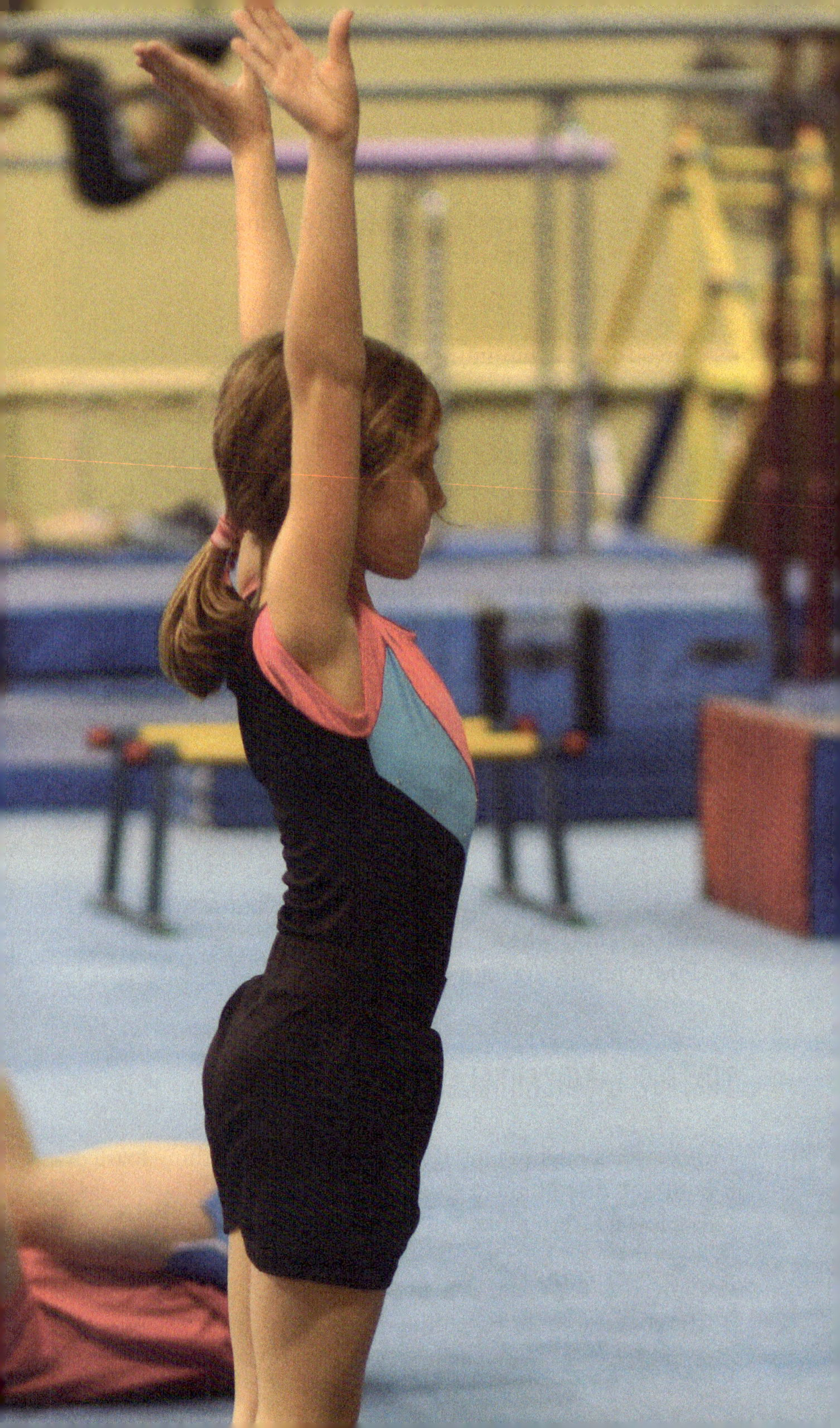

- Put slice of mozzarella in between.

NOTE: *may add basil or fresh tomato slices.*

TURKEY MONTE CRISTO

Makes 4 sandwiches.

8 slices whole-wheat sandwich bread
1 large egg
3 large egg whites
1/4 cup skim milk
Sugar free raspberry or strawberry preserves
8 thin slices low sodium deli turkey
1 cup shredded Swiss cheese

- Preheat oven to 275°F.
- Whisk egg, egg whites, milk, and nutmeg in a shallow dish until combined.
- Spread 1 teaspoon preserves on each slice of bread.
- Put equal amount of turkey and cheese one slice of bread.
- Put 2 tsp preserves on other slice of bread. Close sandwich preserve side down.
- Coat a large nonstick skillet with cooking spray and set heat to medium-low heat.
- Dip 2 sandwiches into the egg mixture, making sure to coat both sides.
- Place the battered sandwiches in the pan, cover and cook until browned and the cheese is melted, 3 to 5 minutes per side.

Best if served warm.

SNACKS

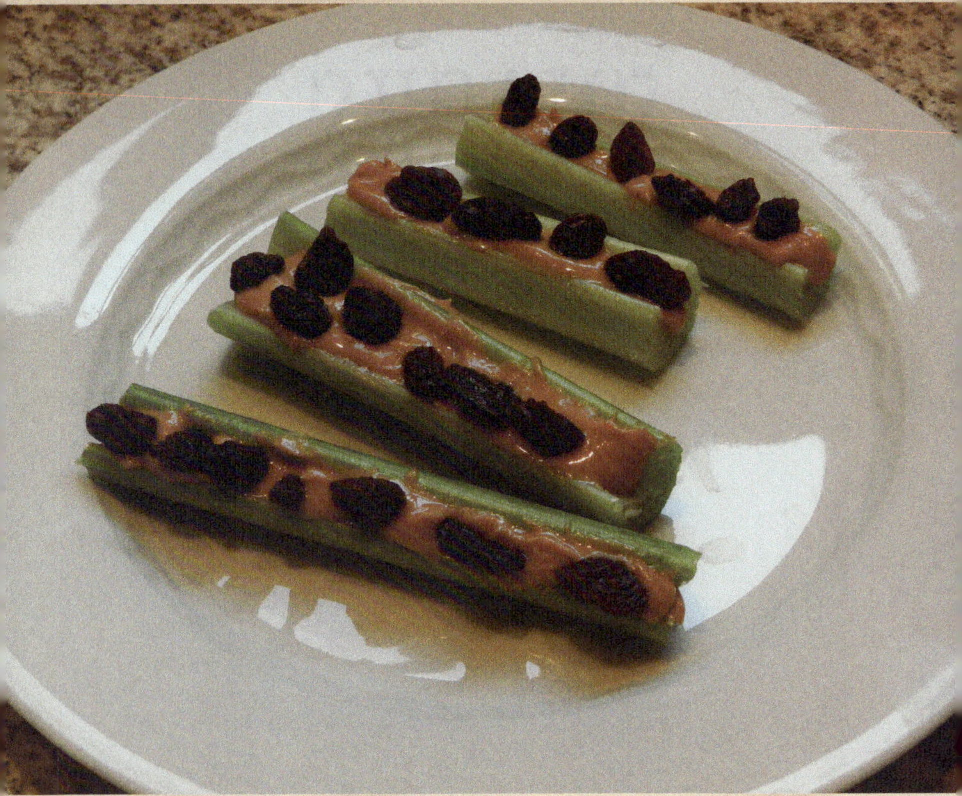

BUGS ON A STICK
Submitted by Eden, age 4

Celery sticks cut in halves
Raisins
Natural creamy peanut butter or PB2 Crunch

- Fill celery sticks with natural peanut butter.
- Add raisins on top of natural peanut butter.

CORN DIP

2 14.5oz cans corn or kernels from fresh boiled corn
1 cup low fat or fat free sour cream
1 cup low fat shredded cheddar
1 TSBP light mayo
1 can diced green chiles
Chopped cilantro – amount to your liking
Salt and pepper to taste
*May add tobasco sauce to taste

Mix all ingredients together in a serving bowl. Serve with pita chips (See recipe this section.)

CUCUMBER BITES

Cucumber slices (can actually use any raw vegetable)
Carton low fat or fat-free plain cream cheese
1 packet dry Ranch or Italian dressing (your choice)

Add dry dressing to taste to cream cheese. (I use about ¼ packet.) Smear onto cucumber slice. May top with shredded carrot or half a cherry tomato.

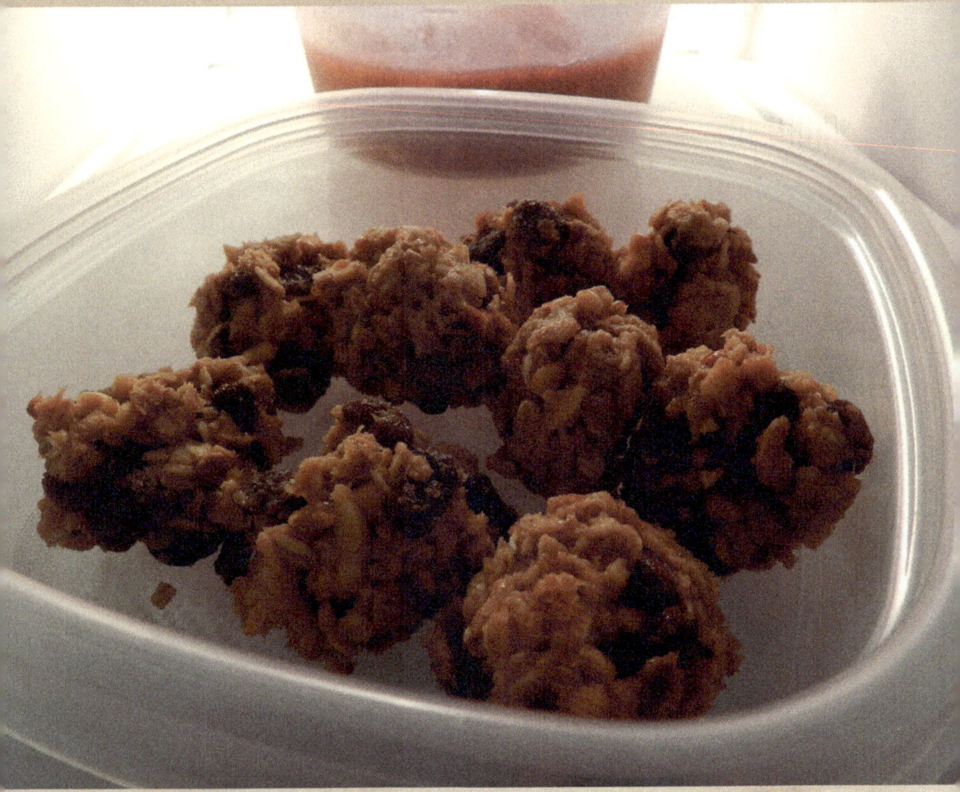

NOTE: I keep a tub of the above "herbed" cream cheese in the fridge and use for additional recipes. You will see it again in other sections of the book.

FRUIT ROLL UPS
Makes 12-14
Recipe from "Get Fit With Nicole"

1 lb fresh berries of your choice
¼ cup agave nectar

- Heat oven to 150.
- Line two baking sheets with wax paper. Grease wax paper with butter.
- If berries have stems, remove stems; wash and dry berries and place in a blender.
- Add agave nectar to strawberries and blend until pureed.
- Spread the mixture evenly on each baking sheet with rubber spatula.
- Place in preheated oven and leave door slightly cracked.
- Allow to dry 7.5 – 10 hours (until no longer sticky).
- Cut in 2" strips and wrap around clean pencils. Place in airtight container.

GRANOLA BITES
Serving size: 3 balls
This recipe is for a large batch. I keep plenty in the freezer at all times. You may cut the recipe down.

1/2 jar chunky natural peanut butter
Unsweetened granola (Add until you get desired consistency. I use about 2 cups.)
Honey or agave nectar (Use until you get desired sweetness – about 1-2 TBSP.)
2 bananas mashed (optional)
2 cups dried fruit (raisins, cranberries, apricots, figs)
Wax paper

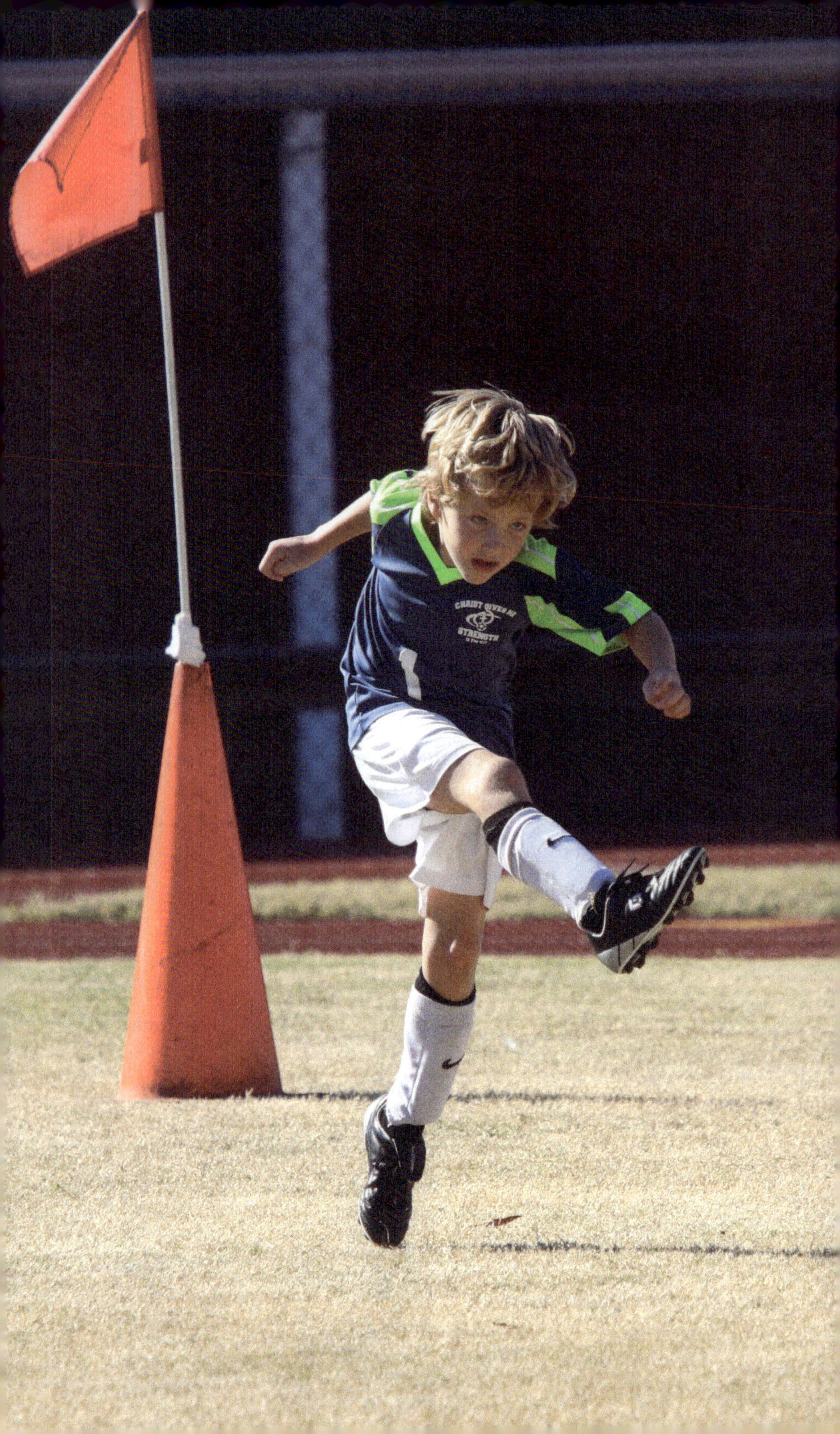

- Mix all ingredients until blended well. I use my hands.
- Roll into 2 inch balls and place on baking pan lined with wax paper.
- Place in freezer 90 minutes or so.
- Keep in freezer and pop them out to fulfill a craving. Eat frozen or let thaw. I keep mine in a Gladware container.

MINI PIZZAS

Whole wheat round crackers (We use Breton.)
Daddy's Marinara (see pg. 87)
Low fat shredded mozzarella
Turkey pepperoni (optional)

- Spread a TBSP of marinara sauce on top of cracker.
- Top with a TBSP of mozzarella cheese.
- Top with 1 turkey pepperoni.
- Pop in microwave 20 seconds if desire or eat as is.

*or create your own combo!

PITA CHIPS

1 Package whole wheat pita bread

- Cut into fourths so they are single layer small triangles.
- Place pita triangles on cookie sheet.
- Bake pita triangles at 350 for 15 minutes.

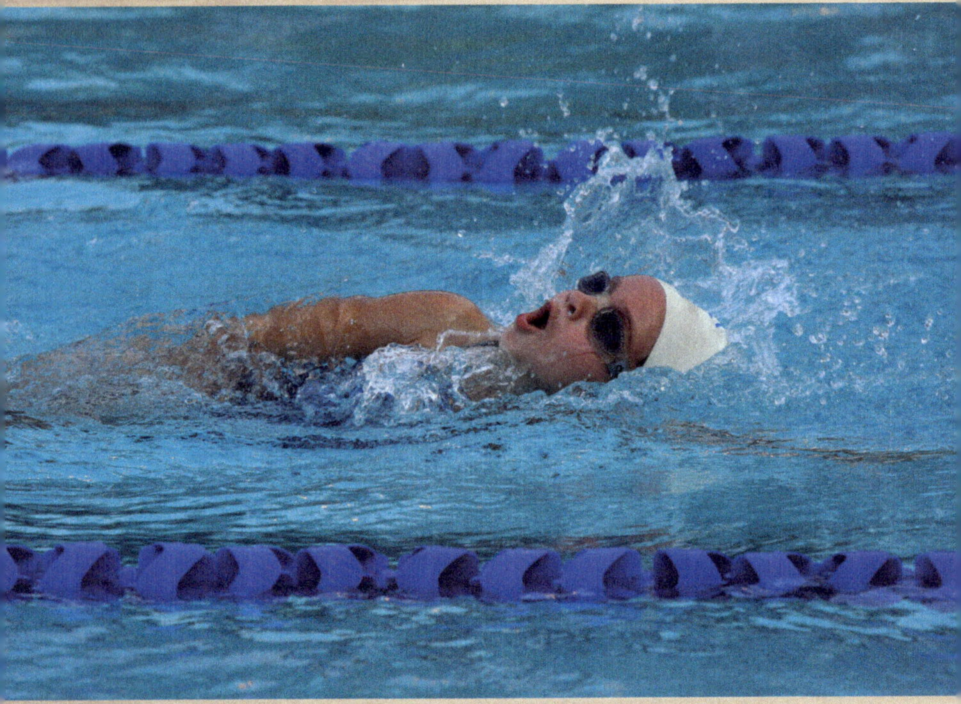

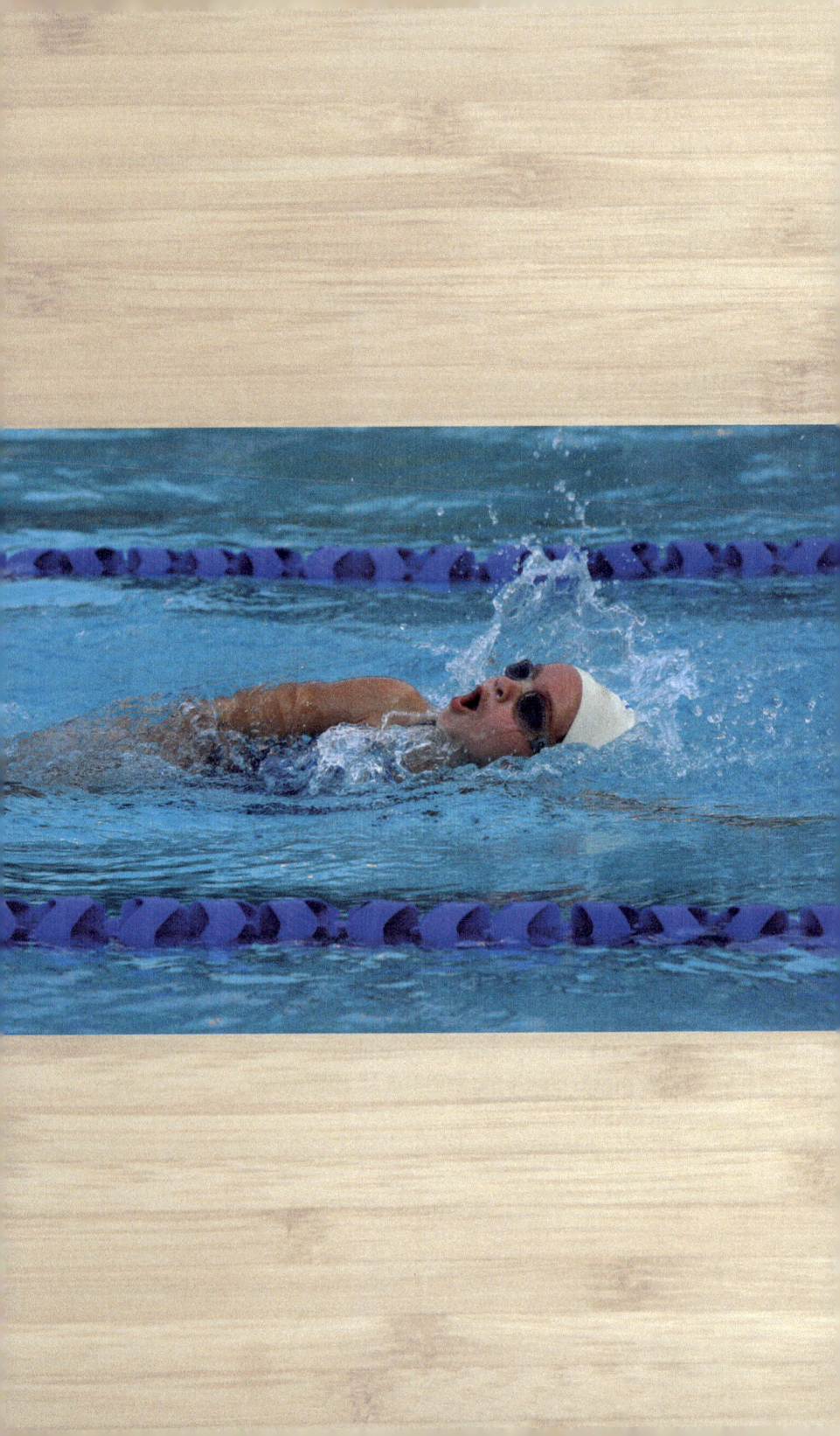

RAINBOW FRUIT SKEWERS

Blunt skewers
Red fruit: we like strawberries.
Orange fruit: we like oranges.
Yellow fruit: we like bananas or star fruit.
Green fruit: we like green grapes or kiwi.
Blue fruit: we like blueberries.
Purple Fruit: we like purple grapes or blackberries.

Stack fruit on skewers in the color order of the rainbow. Enjoy!

Mini version: put three pieces of fruit on popsicle sticks.

SALMON SQUARES

1 whole wheat pizza crust
1 package lox
8oz tub fat free cream cheese
1 packet Ranch dressing
*Optional: fresh dill, chives, red onion

- Cook pizza crust according to directions and allow to cool.
- Add 1-2 TBSP of Ranch packet to tub of cream cheese and stir well.
- Spread cream cheese mixture over cooled pizza crust.
- Add lox on top of cream cheese. (I only use about ¼-1/2 pack.)
- Add "optional" ingredients if choose to.
- Cut into squares and serve.

VEGGIE SQUARES

Use above recipe. Instead of lox, chop your favorite vegetables and sprinkle all over cream cheese to make.

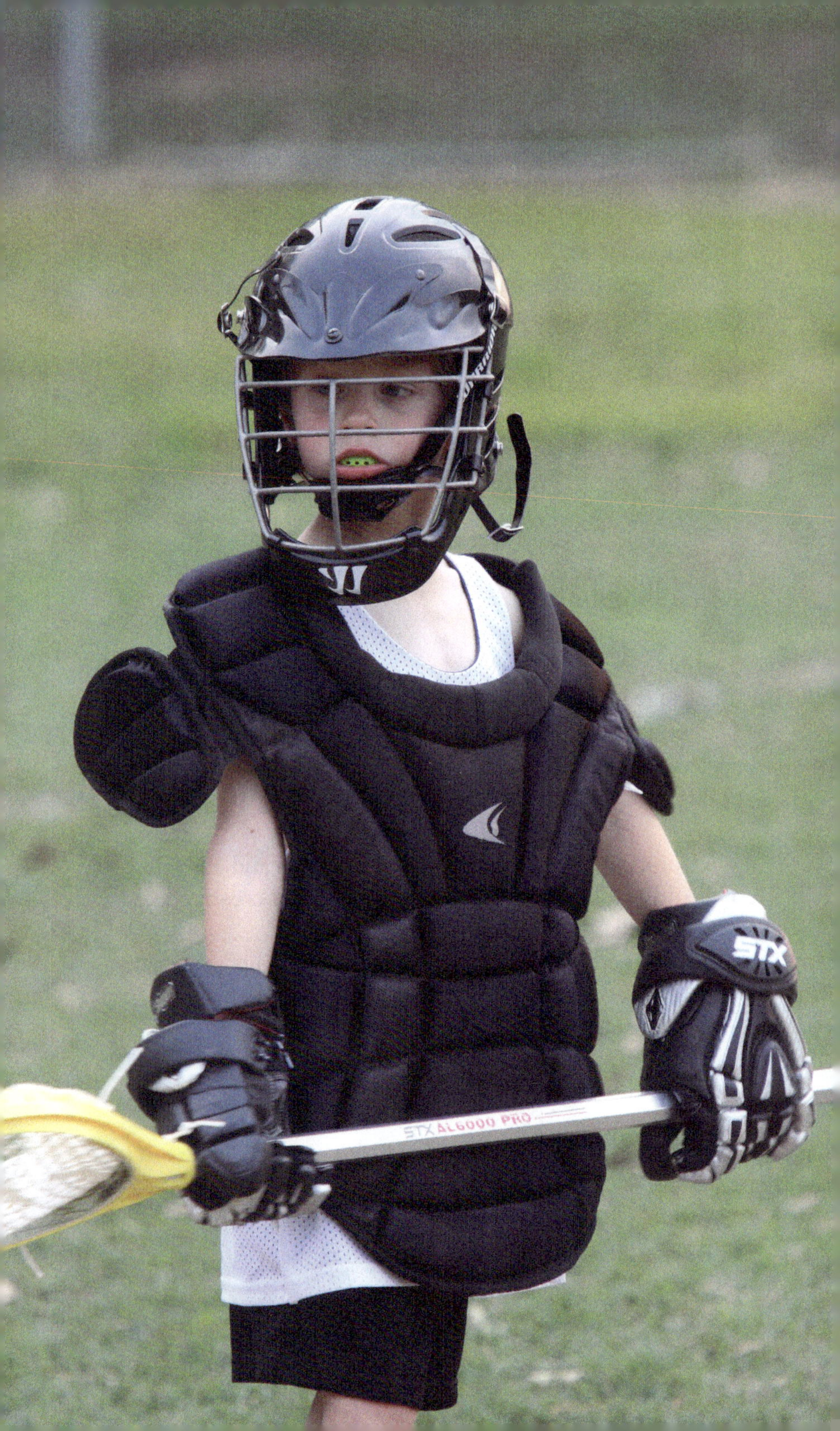
STX
STX AL6000 PRO

SHRIMP DIP
Serving size ¼ cup

1 lb small uncooked shrimp, cut in half to make small pieces
1 red bell pepper diced
1 large carrot finely chopped in food processor/blender (optional)
8oz low fat sour cream
1 cup light mayo
1 cup low fat mozzarella cheese
1 cup shredded parmesan cheese
Salt and pepper to taste
Serve with Pita Chips (see recipe this section)

- Preheat oven 350.
- Mix first 7 (or 8) ingredients in a bowl. Pour into 9x11 casserole dish.
- Bake at 350 for 15 minutes or until bubbly.

SPINACH DIP
Makes 2 cups. Serving size is 1/4 cup.

10 oz fresh baby spinach, steam until wilted
1 cup plain, fat-free yogurt, drained
4oz fat-free cream cheese, softened
¼ cup reduced-fat Parmesan cheese
1 clove garlic, minced
¼ cup scallions, finely chopped
1 TBSP fresh lemon juice
Splash of Tabasco (optional)

- Place spinach in a colander and drain all of the excess water. Finely chop spinach and place in a medium bowl.
- Stir yogurt and cream cheese together until smooth, and then add to the spinach.
- Stir in Parmesan cheese, garlic, scallions, lemon juice, salt, and pepper, and mix well.
- Add Tabasco to taste (optional).
- Refrigerate until ready to serve.

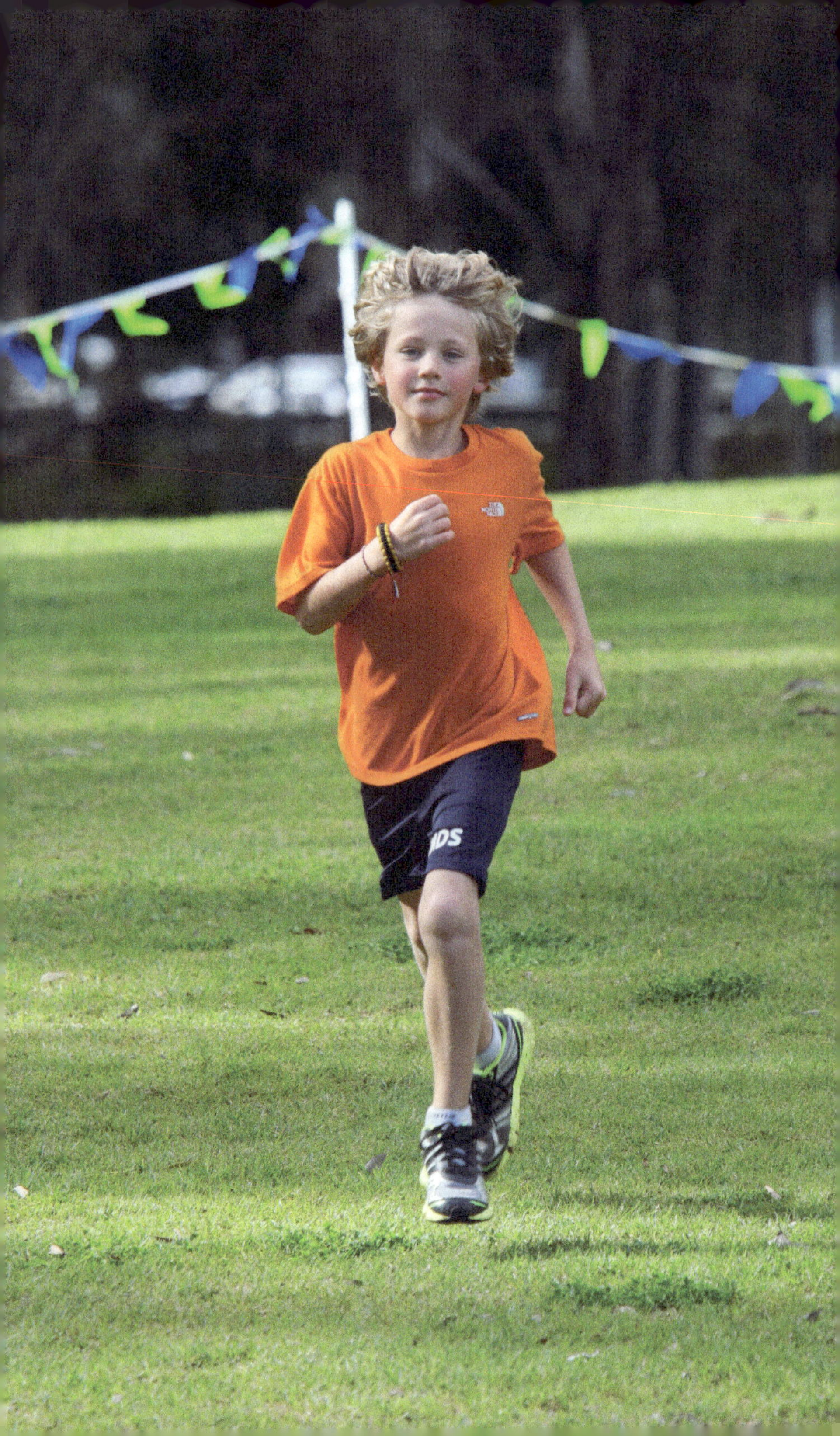

TURKEY TAILS

Whole wheat pita pockets
Fat free hummus
Your favorite vegetables
Cut pita pockets into triangles. Spread fat free hummus on triangles and add chopped vegetables OR use natural peanut butter or PB2 Crunch as the spread and sprinkle chopped apples, celery, or raisins on top.

SNACKS 100 CALORIES OR LESS (FOR PARENTS TOO)

- Fruits
- 1 medium apple
- ¼ cup dried apricots
- 1 small banana
- 1 cup blackberries
- 1 cup blueberries
- 1.5 cups cantelope
- 20 dark red cherries
- ½ cup canned fruit cocktail in juice
- 1 small grapefruit (even with sugar substitute)
- 25 grapes
- 1 cup honeydew melon
- 1 cup mango chunks
- 1 large orange
- ½ cup orange juice
- 1 large peach
- 1 small pear
- 1 cup pineapple
- 1 medium plum
- ½ cup seeds/juice pomegranate
- ¼ cup raisins
- 1 cup raspberries
- 1 cup strawberry halves
- 1 wedge large watermelon

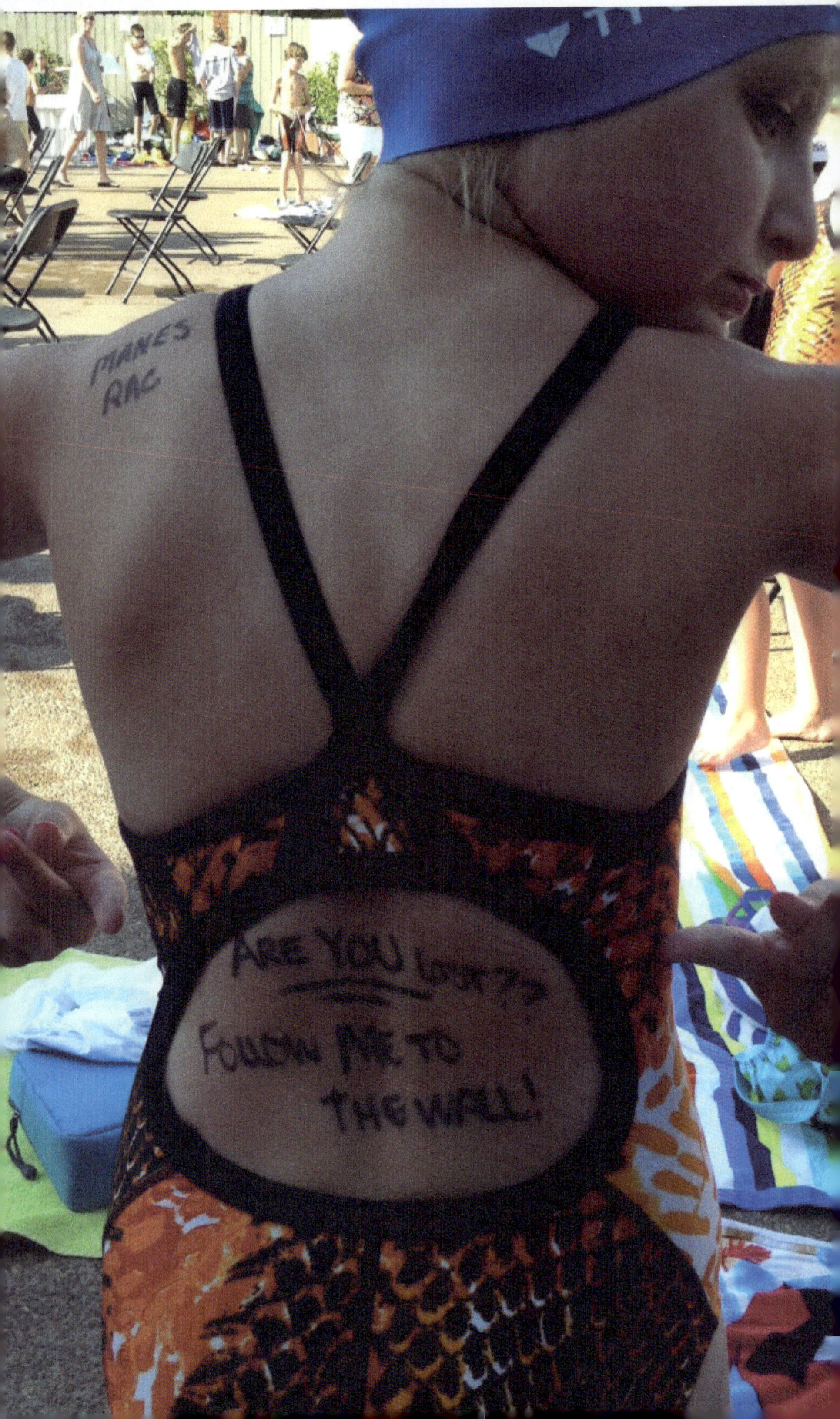
ARE YOU LOST??
FOLLOW ME TO THE WALL!

FRUIT COMBOS

- ¾ cup above fruit choices + 2 TBSP reduced-fat whipped topping
- ½ pear or ½ apple + ½ oz reduced-fat cheddar cheese
- ¼ cup pineapple or pear bits with 1/3 cup 1% cottage cheese
- ½ cup berries with 1/3 cup 1% cottage cheese

VEGETABLES

- 45 steamed edamame
- 1 cup low-sodium vegetable juice
- 12 baby carrots
- 1 cup cauliflower
- 18 small celery sticks
- 1 medium corn on the cob + ½ tsp butter
- 1 cucumber sliced
- 1 cup cherry or grape tomatoes
- 2 cups raw vegetables
- 2 cups raw sugar snap peas

VEGGIE COMBOS

- Any of the above vegetables + 2 TBSP fat free salad dressing
- ½ red bell pepper sliced or above raw vegetables + 3 TBSP fat-free hummus
- 2 medium celery sticks with 1 TBSP reduced-fat cream cheese
- 2 TBSP mashed avocado + 2 TBSP chopped tomato in ½ mini whole wheat pita
- 1/2 to 1 cup raw vegetables + 2 TBSP reduced-fat feta cheese + 2 TBSP fat-free dressing wrapped in a lettuce leaf
- 2 cups fresh spinach + 1 cup shredded carrots (or any raw vegetable) + 2 TBSP fat-free dressing
- 2 pieces California rolls
- Bugs on a Stick (see recipe in Snack section)

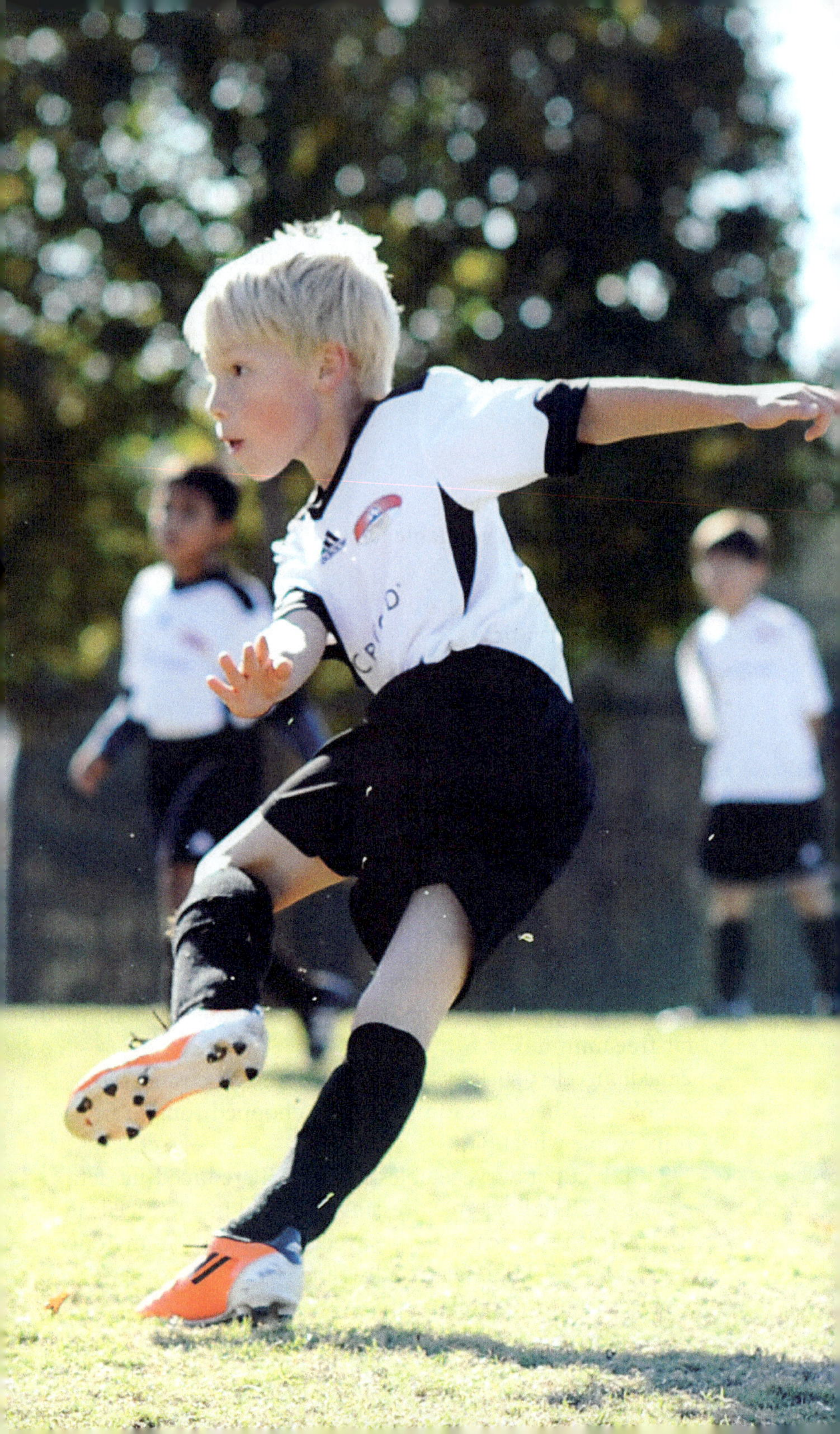

DAIRY

- 1 oz reduced-fat cheddar cheese
- ½ cup chocolate soy milk
- ½ cup low-fat cottage cheese
- 2 Laughing Cow Light cheese wedges
- 2 Sargento string cheese sticks
- 1 large hardboiled egg
- 1 cup fat-free milk
- 6oz container fat-free yogurt
- ¾ cup sugar-free cocoa (with skim milk)

GRAINS, ETC.

- 100 calorie popcorn snack bags
- 10 organic whole wheat pretzel sticks
- 100 calorie pack Goldfish
- ½ whole wheat English muffin with fruit preserves
- 2 brown rice cakes (or rice cakes)
- ¼ cup unsalted peanuts (150 calories)
- 1/3 cup sunflower seeds
- 1/3 cup pumpkin seeds
- 3 TBSP soy nuts
- 1 Nutri Grain whole wheat waffle with ¼ cup sugar-free syrup
- ½ whole wheat bagel thin with 2 TBSP PB2 Crunch
- ½ whole wheat bagel thin with 1 TBSP fat-free hummus
- Fresh spinach + 2 TSBP fat-free hummus + ½ of whole wheat pita (can add tomato slices, shredded carrots or sprouts)
- 1 slice turkey + ½ TBSP low fat cream cheese + ½ of mini whole wheat pita
- 10 whole wheat Wheat Thins
- 1 slice whole wheat bread with 2 TBSP PB2 Crunch
- 10 baked tortilla chips with salsa
- 4 Breton whole wheat crackers
- 20 Special K cracker chips

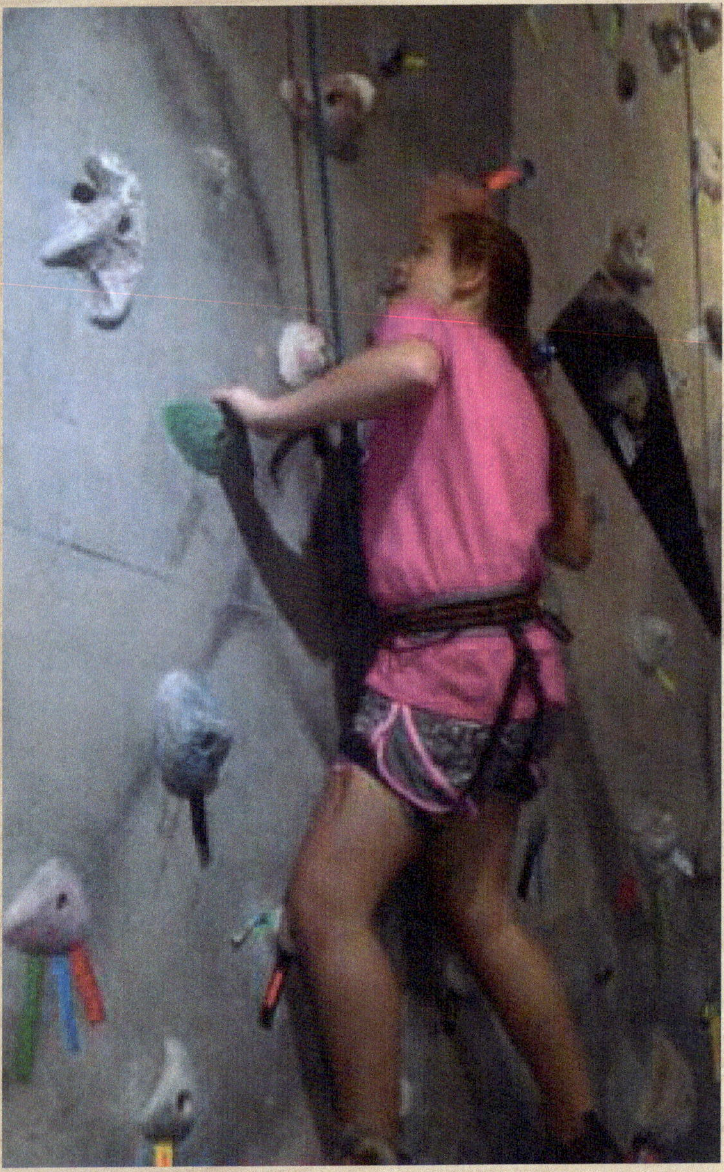

SWEETS (IF YOU MUST)

- 5 Nabisco Nilla wafers
- 1 cup sugar-free Jell-O
- ½ cup sugar-free pudding
- 4 Hersey Kisses
- 3 graham crackers
- 100 calorie snack packs of cookies, etc
- 9 mini tootsie rolls
- Skinny Cow or Weight Watchers ice cream bars (check label)
- Twix 90 cal ice cream minis
- 2 gingersnaps with a smear low fat cream cheese (can do flavored)
- 1 rice crispy treat
- ½ cup sherbet or sorbet

www.tasteofhome.com
www.caloriecount.about.com
www.nhlbi.nih.gov/health/public/heart/obesity

SWEET TOOTH

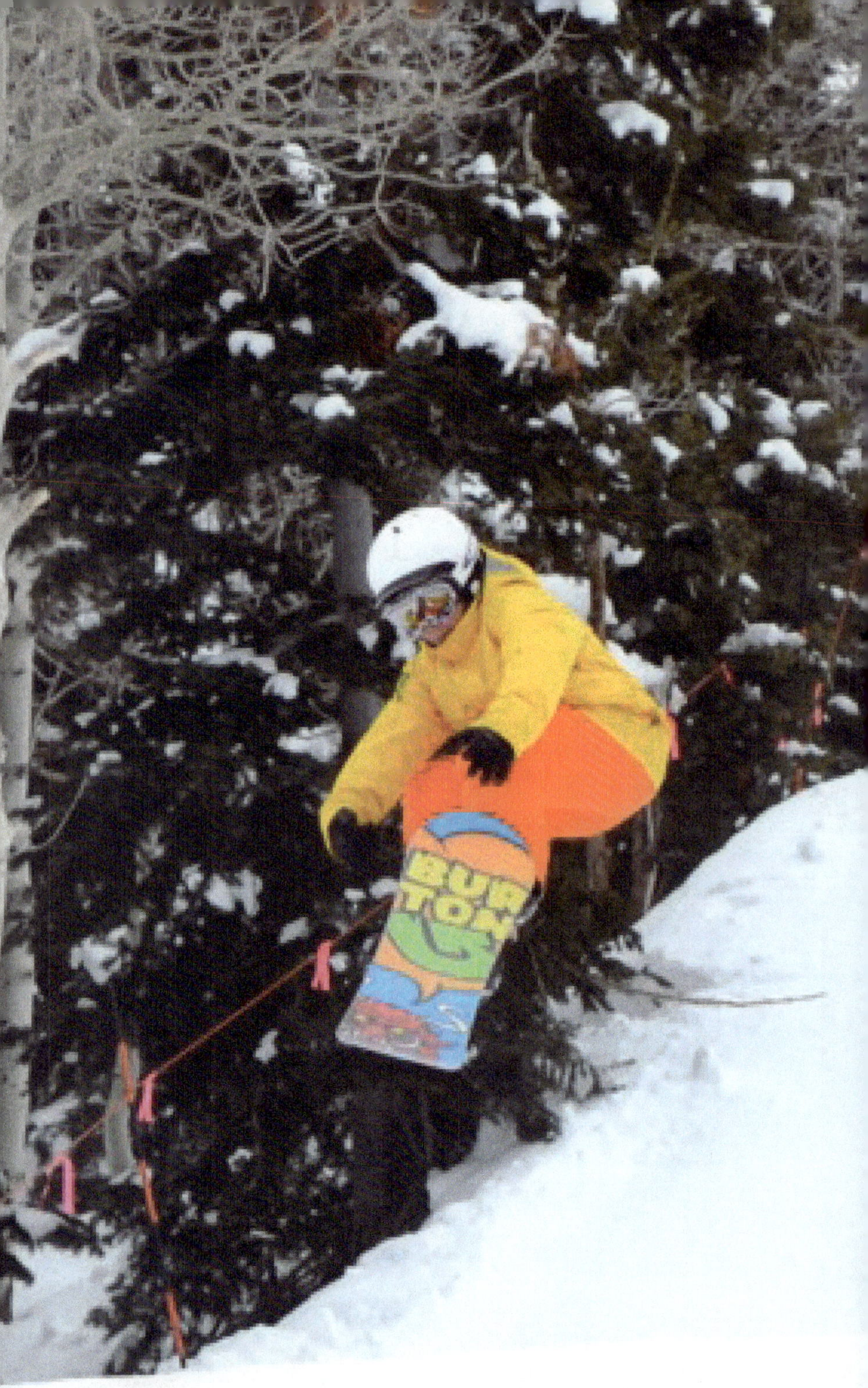
BUR
TON

CONVERSION CHART FOR SUGAR SUBSTITUTES

	Ratio to refined sugar	Comments
Agave Nectar	Multiply amount of sugar x 2/3 = amount of agave	Decrease liquids in recipes by ¼ to 1/3 for every 2/3 cup agave
Erythritol	1:1	May increase amount according to your taste
Honey	Multiply amount of sugar x 2/3 = amount of honey	
Stevia liquid	1 tsp:1 cup sugar	
Stevia powder	1:1	Add 10% liquid in recipes
Splenda granulated	1:1	
Splenda sugar blend	½:1	
Splenda brown sugar blend	½:1 (to substitute for brown sugar)	
Xylitol	1:1	May decrease amount according to your taste as xylitol is sweet

I primarily use agave nectar and Xylitol.

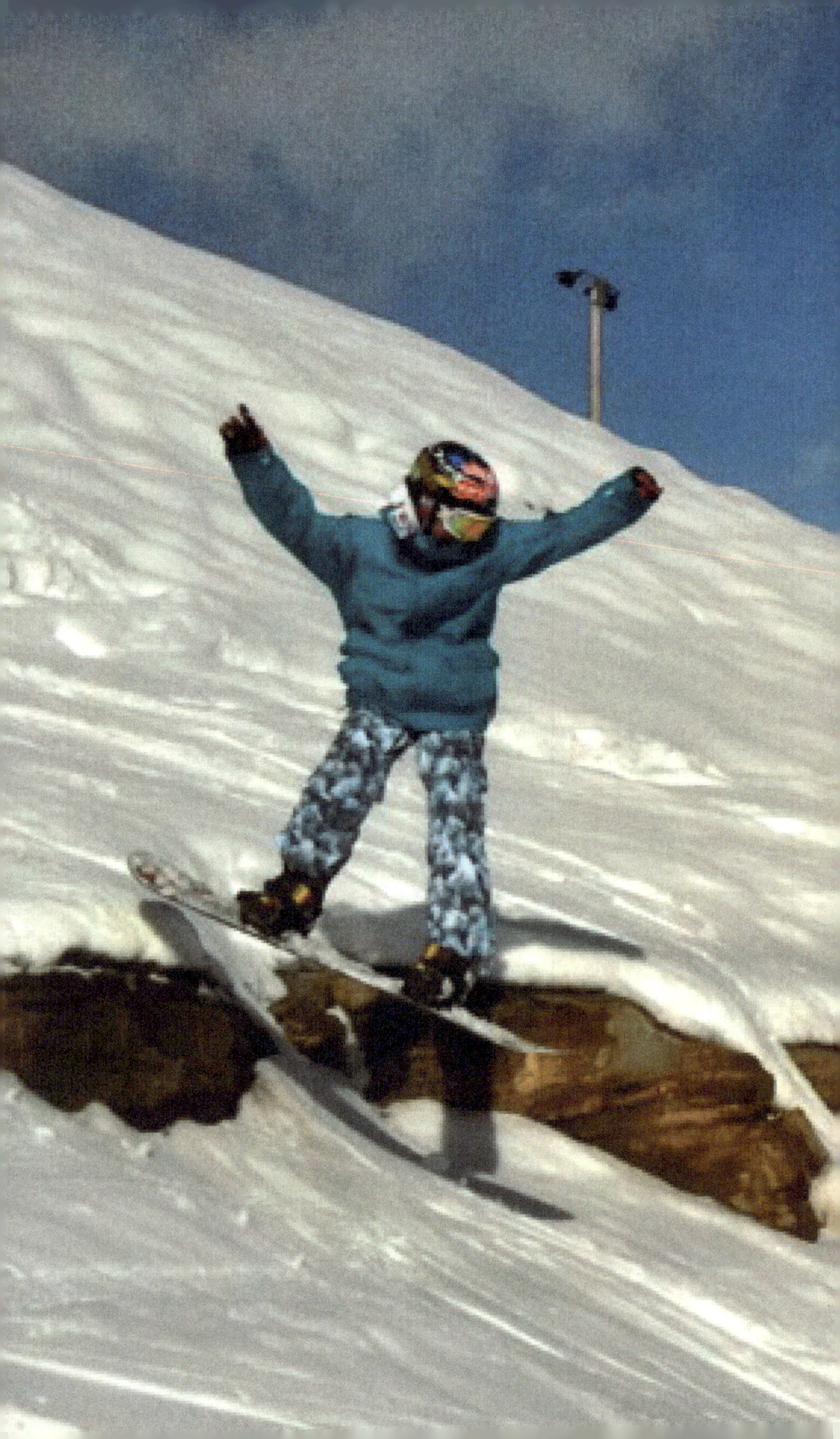

BANANA SPLIT

2 large bananas peeled and halved
1 cup strawberries
Sugar free caramel ice cream topping
Sugar free chocolate ice cream topping
Fat-free whipped topping

- Cut banana halves in slices and put into 4 small serving bowl.
- Put ¼ cup strawberries in each serving bowl with bananas.
- Drizzle with caramel sauce, chocolate sauce or both!
- Top with a TBSP fat free whipped topping.

Feel free to add ¼ cup blueberries to bananas and strawberries also.

BANANA PUDDING
Kaitlin Moore, 9 years old

2 large boxes of sugar free vanilla instant pudding
3 cups skim milk
8 ounces low-fat sour cream
24 ounces cool whip (light, fat free, or sugar free your choice)
7 large ripe bananas
1 1/2 bags of Jackson's vanilla wafers

- Blend first 3 ingredients in a large bowl.
- Add 1/3-1/2 of the cool whip, blend, and set in fridge (basically to your taste).
- Peel and slice bananas.
- Alternate layers of wafers, bananas, and pudding (always nice in a trifle bowl but any dish will work).
- Top with cool whip and sprinkle with wafer crumbs.

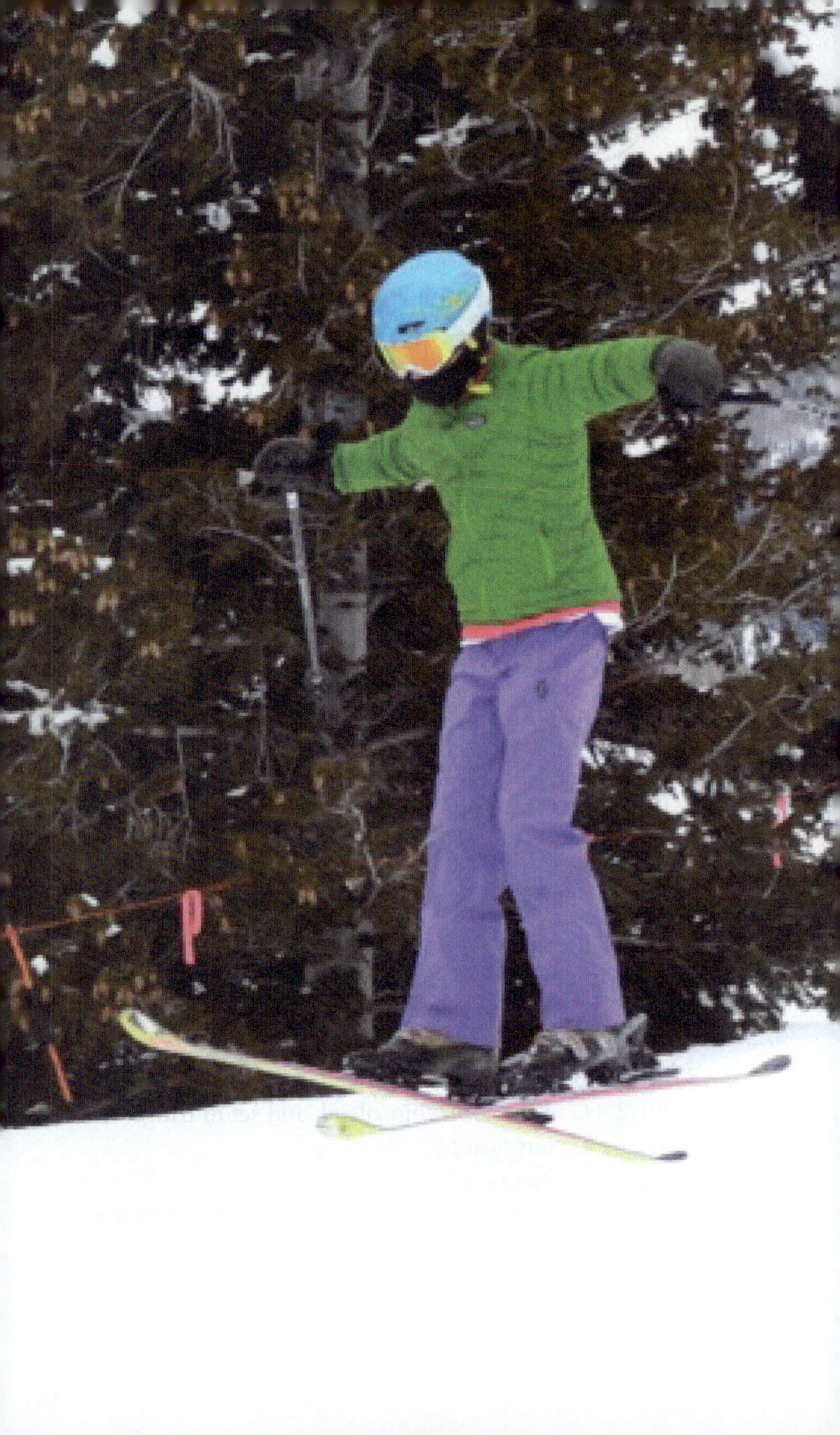

BREAD PUDDING
Makes 6 servings

8 slices whole wheat bread (toasted and cut into 4 squares or 4 triangles
Sugar substitute for ¼ cup sugar (see conversion chart)
1 tsp cinnamon
2 cups low-fat milk
4 eggs or 2 whole eggs, 3 egg whites
1 TBSP brown sugar substitute
1.5 tsp vanilla extract
Sugar free caramel topping

- Preheat oven to 375.
- Mix sugar substitute and cinnamon in small bowl.
- In separate bowl, whisk the milk, eggs, brown sugar substitute, and vanilla.
- Layer half the bread in the bottom of a 9x9 baking dish.
- Sprinkle with half the cinnamon and sugar substitute mixture.
- Repeat with a second layer of bread then cinnamon and sugar mixture.
- Pour milk mixture over entire dish.
- Bake 40-50 minutes.
- Drizzle caramel sauce over each serving.

BROWNIES
Makes 6 servings

There were so many brownie recipes involving whole wheat flour, cocoa, and applesauce when I needed one 6 months ago that I do not recall which site I got this from.

7 TBSPs whole wheat flour (can do ½ whole wheat ½ white for longevity)
1/2 cup cocoa
1/4 tsp salt

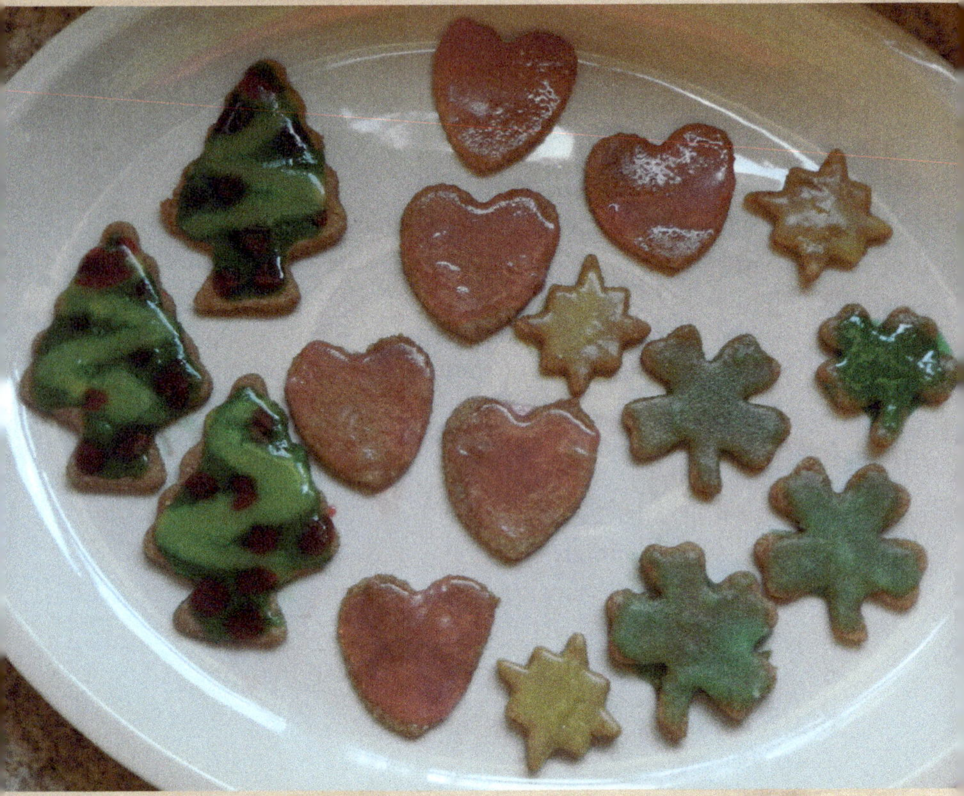

2 egg whites
1 egg
Sugar substitute for ¾ cups sugar (I use ¼ cup agave nectar and ½ tsp stevia)
8 TBSP applesauce
1 TBSP oil
1.5 tsp pure vanilla extract

- Preheat oven 350.
- Combine first 3 ingredients.
- Whisk egg whites, egg, sugar substitute, applesauce, oil, and vanilla.
- Add egg mixture to flour mixture just until blended.
- Pour into 8x8 greased pan.
- Bake 25 minutes.

*if want to add chocolate icing, see chocolate cake recipe this section OR use sugar free can icing.

MOM'S BUTTER COOKIES
(also used for sugar cookies)

Sift together:
3 cups whole wheat flour (if you want these to last more than a day, use ½ whole wheat flour ½ white flour)
1 tsp baking powder
½ tsp salt

Cream in mixer:
1 cup unsalted butter softened
1 cup sugar substitute (Xylitol or granulated splenda)

Add in:
1 egg
2 TBSP skim milk
1.5 tsp pure vanilla extract

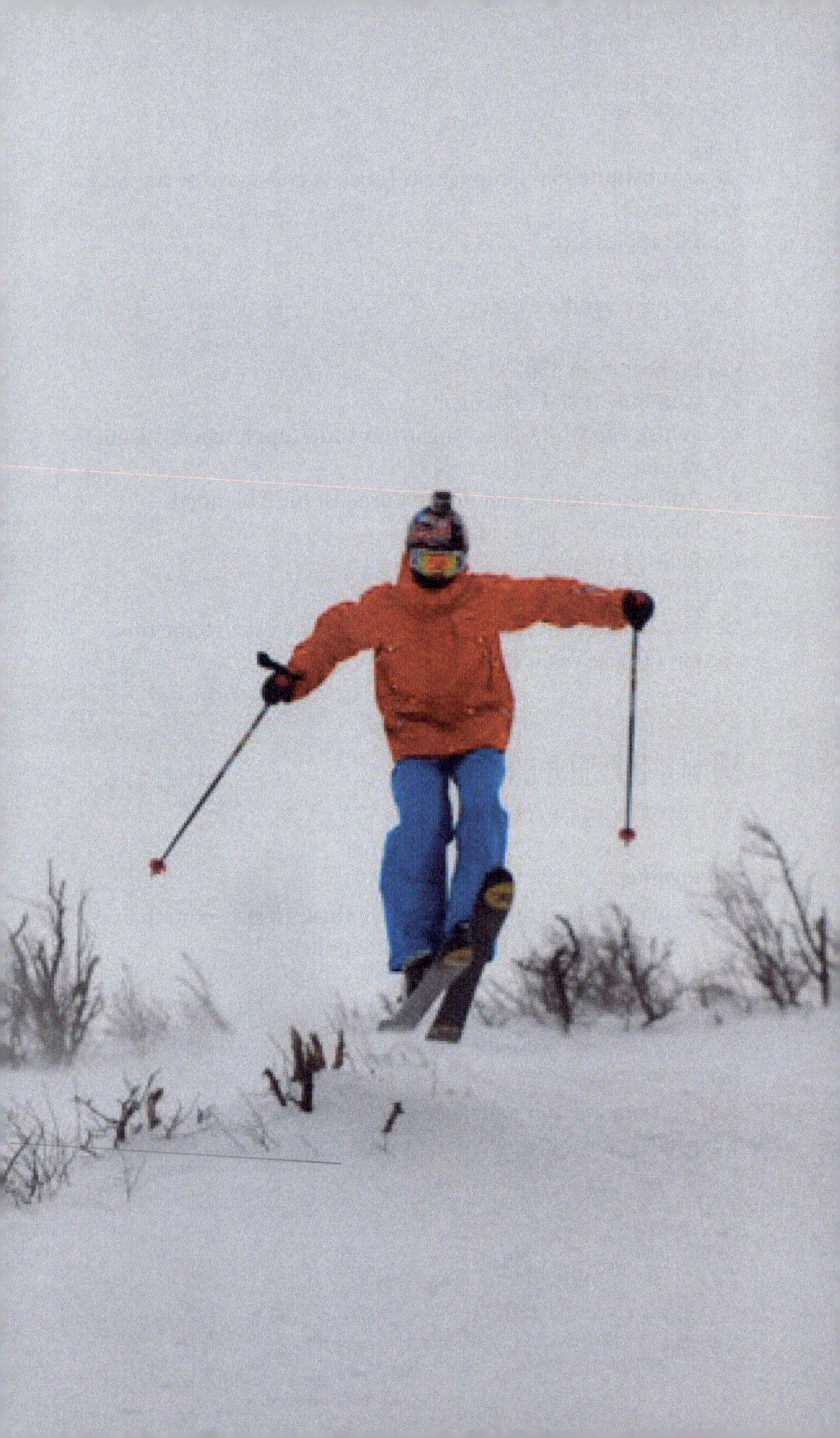

- Beat well and blend in dry ingredients. Wrap in plastic wrap and chill for one hour.
- Bake 350 5-8 minute.

Butter cookie icing:
¼ cup boiling water
1 tsp butter
1-2 cups powdered sugar. See recipe (if not using recipe, need to sift).

- Bring water and butter to a boil.
- Remove from heat.
- Stir in powdered sugar until achieve desired consistency (1-2 cups).
- May add food coloring.

CHEESECAKE

Crust:
½ box whole wheat graham crackers (if can't find whole wheat, use 1 cup Kashi cereal (or comparable)+ ½ cup low fat graham crackers)
½ cup almonds
1/3 cup oil (coconut, canola or vegetable)
1 TBSP unsalted butter, melted

- Put graham crackers and almonds in food processor/blender until fine crumbs.
- Pour in bowl. Add oil and butter.
- Mix with hands or spoon until well blended.
- Press into bottom of 9" pie pan.

Filling:
2 8oz packages low fat cream cheese
2 cups vanilla Greek yogurt
1 tsp pure vanilla extract
6 tsp powdered sugar (see recipe this section for "Powdered Sugar")

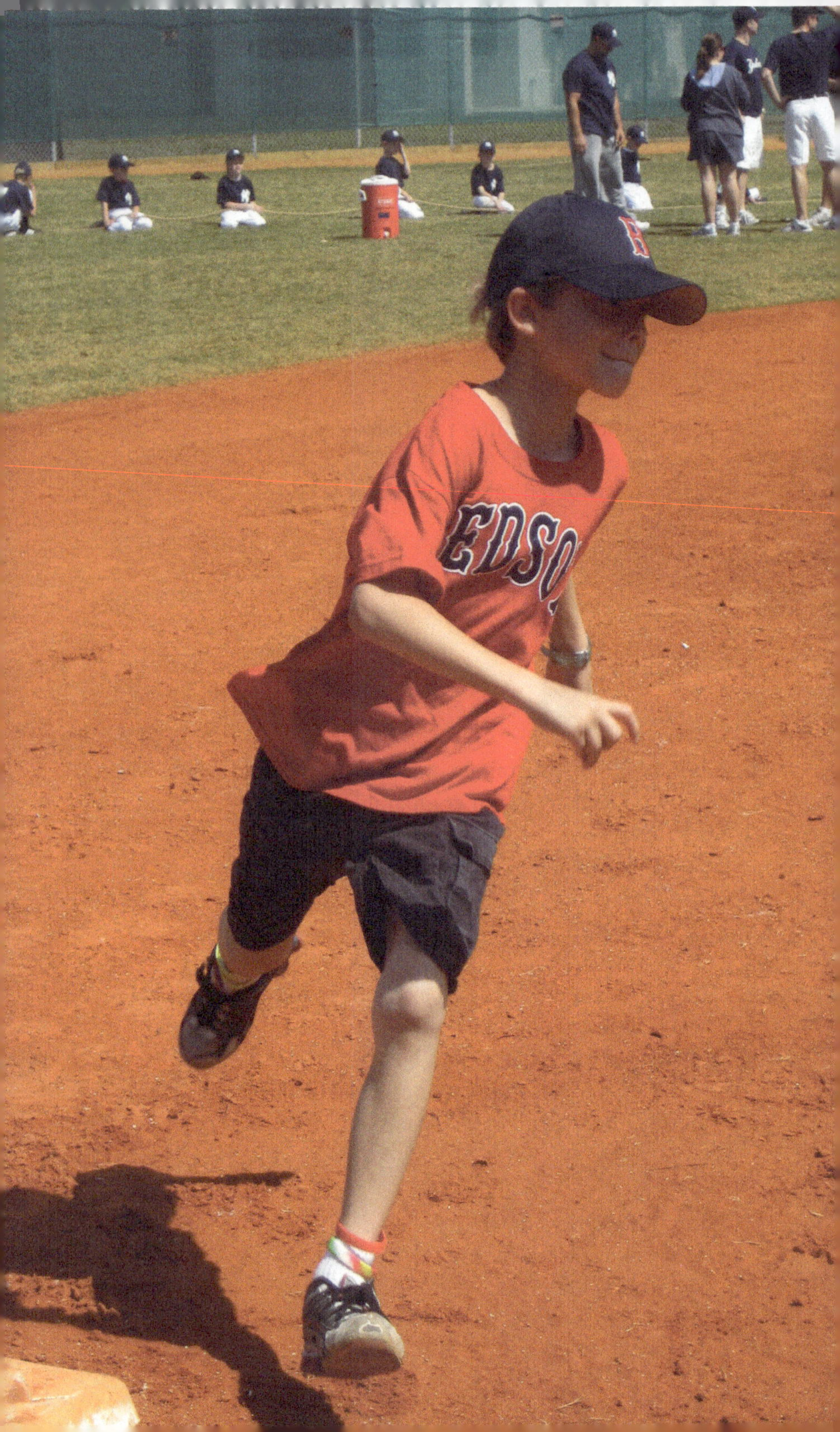

- Beat all ingredients in electric mixer.
- Pour over pie crust.
- Refrigerate until set (about 3 hours).

Top with fresh berries (optional).

CHOCOLATE CAKE
(also for cupcakes)
Adapted from www.healthyindulgences.com

Pillsbury sugar free chocolate cake mix
OR
This recipe… I first saw this actual cake at a friend's workplace. It looked so great I had to try it. I adapted the recipe from www.healthyindulgences.com
Allow 24 hours to sit. Recipe is for a single layer cake.

1-15 ounce can of unseasoned black beans, rinsed and drained
5 large eggs
Sugar substitute for 1 cup sugar (I use ½ cup agave nectar + ½ tsp stevia)
1 tablespoon pure vanilla extract
1/2 teaspoon sea salt
6 tablespoons unsalted butter
6 tablespoons unsalted butter
1/2 teaspoon stevia extract
6 tablespoons unsweetened cocoa powder
1 teaspoon baking powder
1/2 teaspoon baking soda
1 tablespoon water
2oz unsweetened chocolate (optional)
2 TBSP unsalted butter (optional)

- Preheat oven to 325 degrees.
- Place beans, 3 eggs, vanilla, stevia, and salt into food

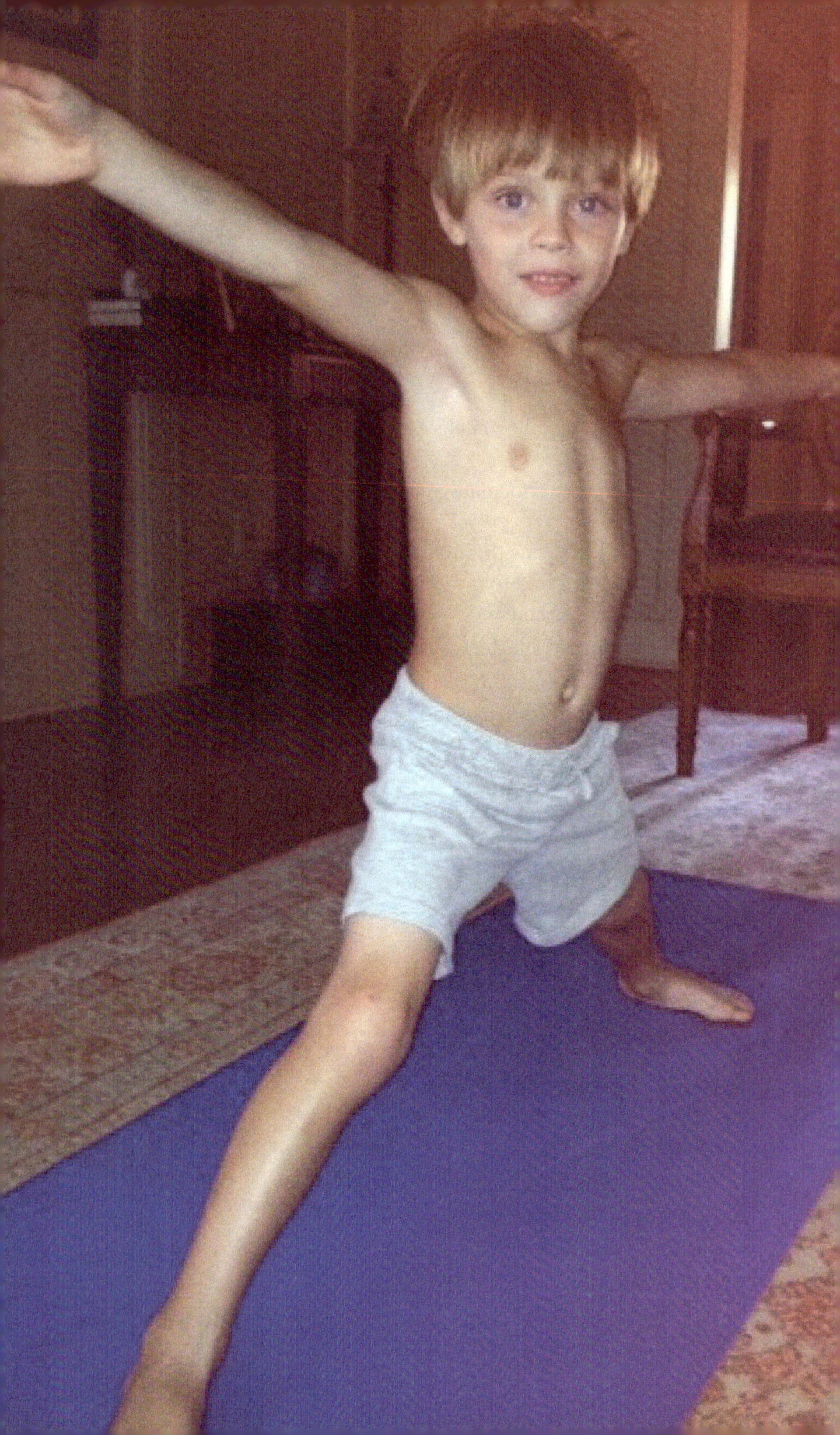

processor/blender. Blend on high until beans are completely liquefied without lumps.
- Whisk together cocoa powder, baking soda, and baking powder.
- Beat butter with sugar substitute until smooth.
- Add remaining two eggs, beating for 2 minutes.
- Pour bean batter into egg mixture and mix.
- Stir in cocoa powder and water. Beat the batter on high until smooth.
- For extra chocolate, melt unsweetened chocolate with butter in microwave. Stir in 1-2 TBSP granulated sugar substitute. Add to batter.

*If using as cake, prep pan: grease or spray pan; dust with cocoa covering bottom of pan discarding excess.
*If plan on removing cake from cake pan to layer and/or ice, lace pan on wax paper and trace around with a toothpick. Cut out pan shape and line bottom of pan.
OR
*If making cupcakes, spray cupcake liners with cooking spray and spoon batter into cupcake liners until full.

- Bake for 40-45 minutes.
- Once cooled, flip over onto a plate and cover in plastic wrap and let cake sit over night or leave in pan if serving from baking pan.

Chocolate Icing recipe below under Cola Cake

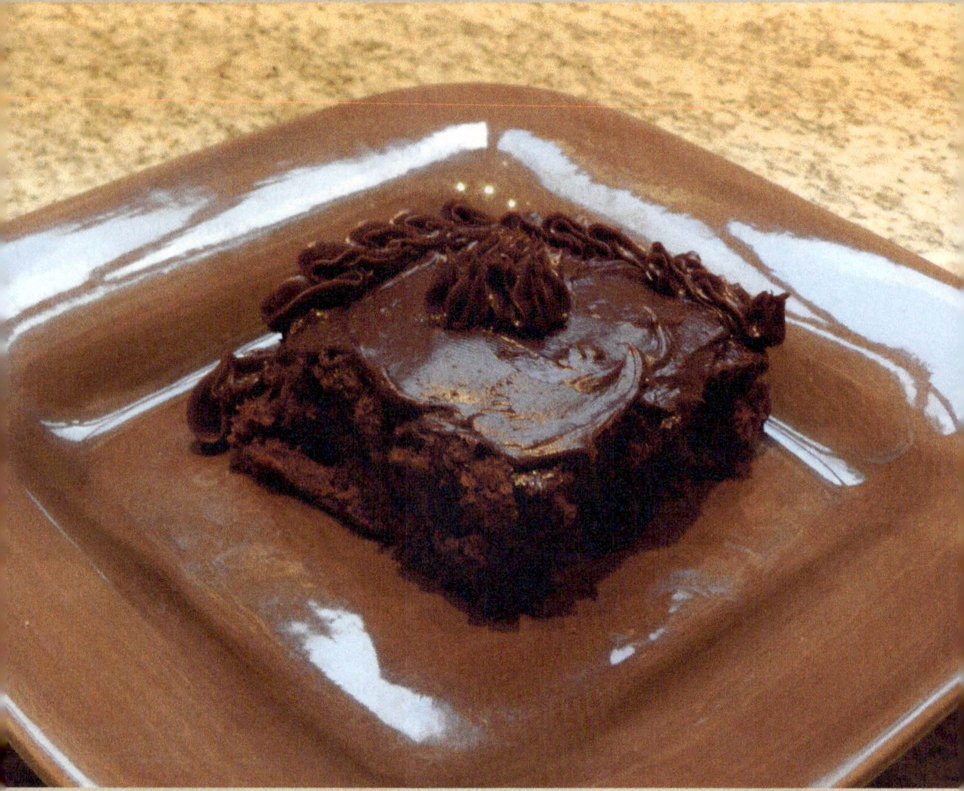

NANA'S COLA CAKE
(adapted from The Diabetic Pastry Chef)

1 box Pillsbury sugar free Devil's Food cake mix
10 oz Coke zero

- Mix both ingredients and pour into a 9x13 greased baking pan.
- Bake 350 according to package directions.

Chocolate Icing:
1 cup unsalted butter
¼ tsp salt
2 cups powdered sugar (see recipe this section)
1 box sugar free chocolate pudding OR ½ cup cocoa
¼ cup skim milk
1 tsp pure vanilla extract

- Cream butter and salt in mixer.
- Gradually add in powdered sugar and pudding/cocoa.
- Gradually add milk and vanilla.
- Blend well until icing forms.

CHOCOLATE CHIP COOKIES

¼ cup light salted butter
½ tsp vanilla
1 cup whole wheat flour (use ½ whole wheat, ½ white for longevity)
2 tsp baking powder
4 tsp liquid sweetener (stevia, agave or honey)
1 egg
½ tsp salt
¼ tsp soda
½ cup sugar free chocolate (semi sweet choc chips, dairy free or equivalent)

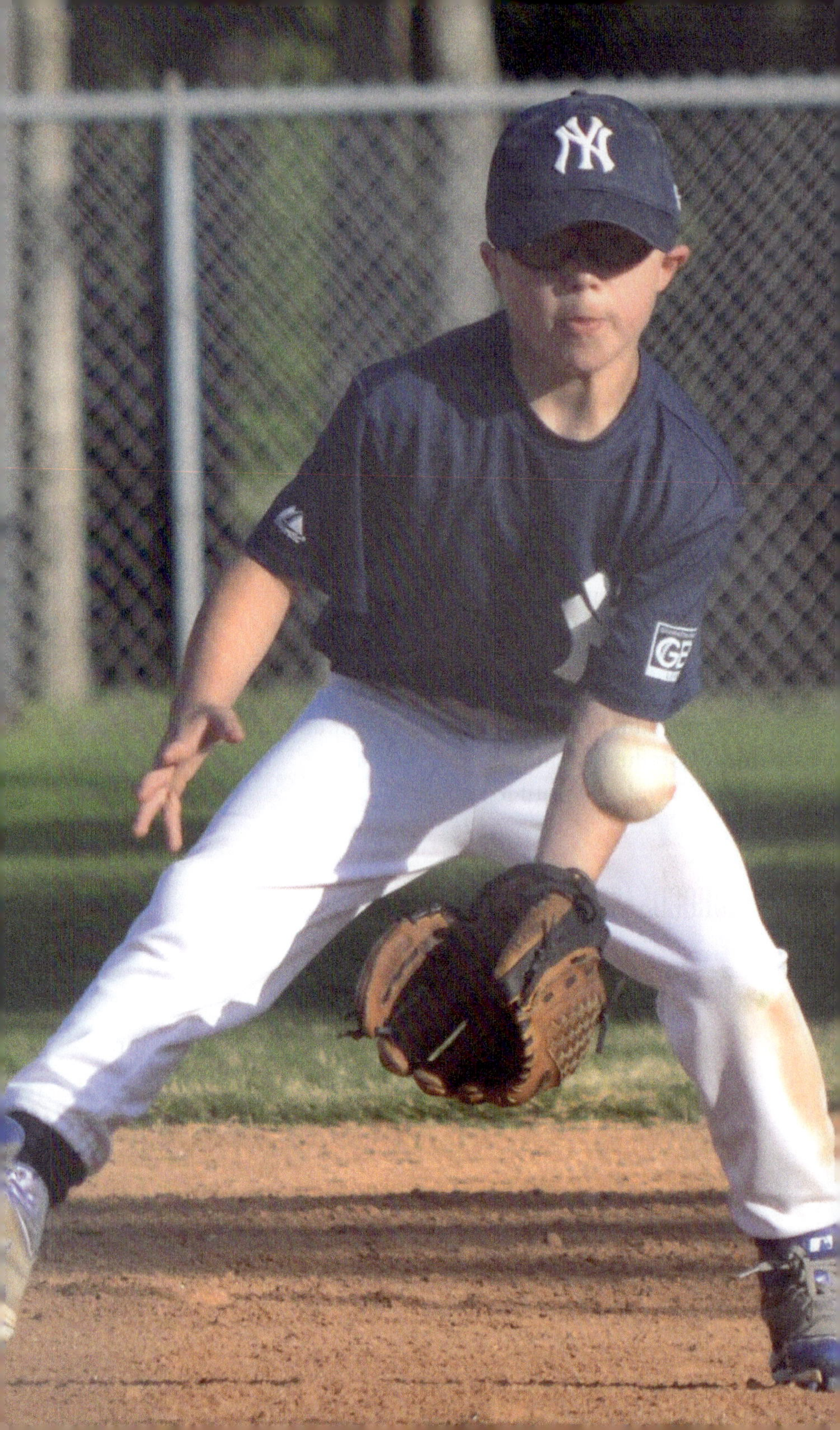

- Combine first four ingredients in a mixing bowl. Beat at high speed 1-2 minutes.
- Add next four ingredients with ½ cup water. Blend low speed.
- Stir in chocolate chips.
- Scoop in spoonfuls onto baking sheet.
- Bake 450 for 10-12 min.

FRUIT COBBLER

Makes 6 servings

Topping:

Sugar substitute for ¼ cup sugar (see conversion chart)
3 low fat graham crackers
¼ cup unsalted butter
2 TBSP whole wheat flour
1 tsp cinnamon

Place all ingredients in a food processor/blender. Blend until crumbly. Set aside.

Filling:

3 of the following fruits peeled and sliced (pick one or use combination):
- Pears
- Peaches
- Apples

2 TBSP whole wheat flour
Sugar substitute for ¼ cup sugar (see conversion chart)
1 TBSP lemon juice
3 TBSP water
½ tsp cinnamon

- Preheat oven to 350.
- Mix all filling ingredients together. Place in 8x8 coated baking pan.
- Cover with topping.
- Bake at 350 for 40-45 minutes or until bubbly.

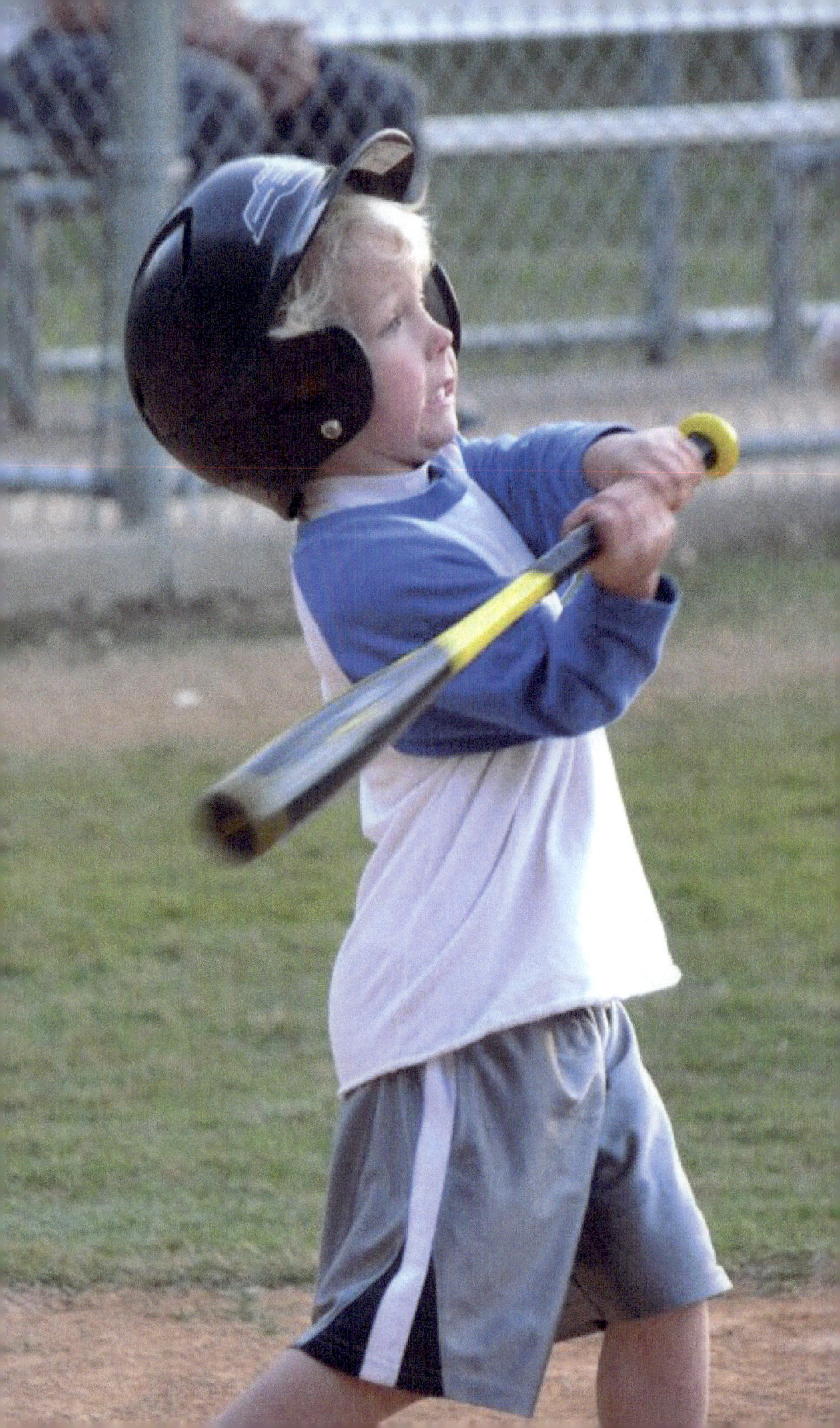

GRAPE DESSERT

Kaitlin Moore, 9 years old: "My Mom and I enjoy making this together. I wash the grapes while she mixes the other ingredients."

1 bag of green grapes
1 bag of red seedless grapes
8 ounces low-fat sour cream
8 ounces low-fat cream cheese (softened)
1/3 cup brown sugar (to taste)
1 tsp. vanilla

- Wash your grapes and have an adult cut them in half if needed.
- Using a mixer, mix together sour cream, cream cheese, brown sugar, and vanilla.
- Sometimes there is more mixture than I need, so I put my grapes in their serving bowl and add the mix to them.
- Optional: Sprinkle with brown sugar and chopped walnuts or pecans.

This is also a nice spring/summer side dish as well as brunch and Easter.
Enjoy!

POWDERED SUGAR

1 cup granulated Xylitol or granulated Splenda
1-2 tablespoons cornstarch

Blend on high in blender until powdery and light.

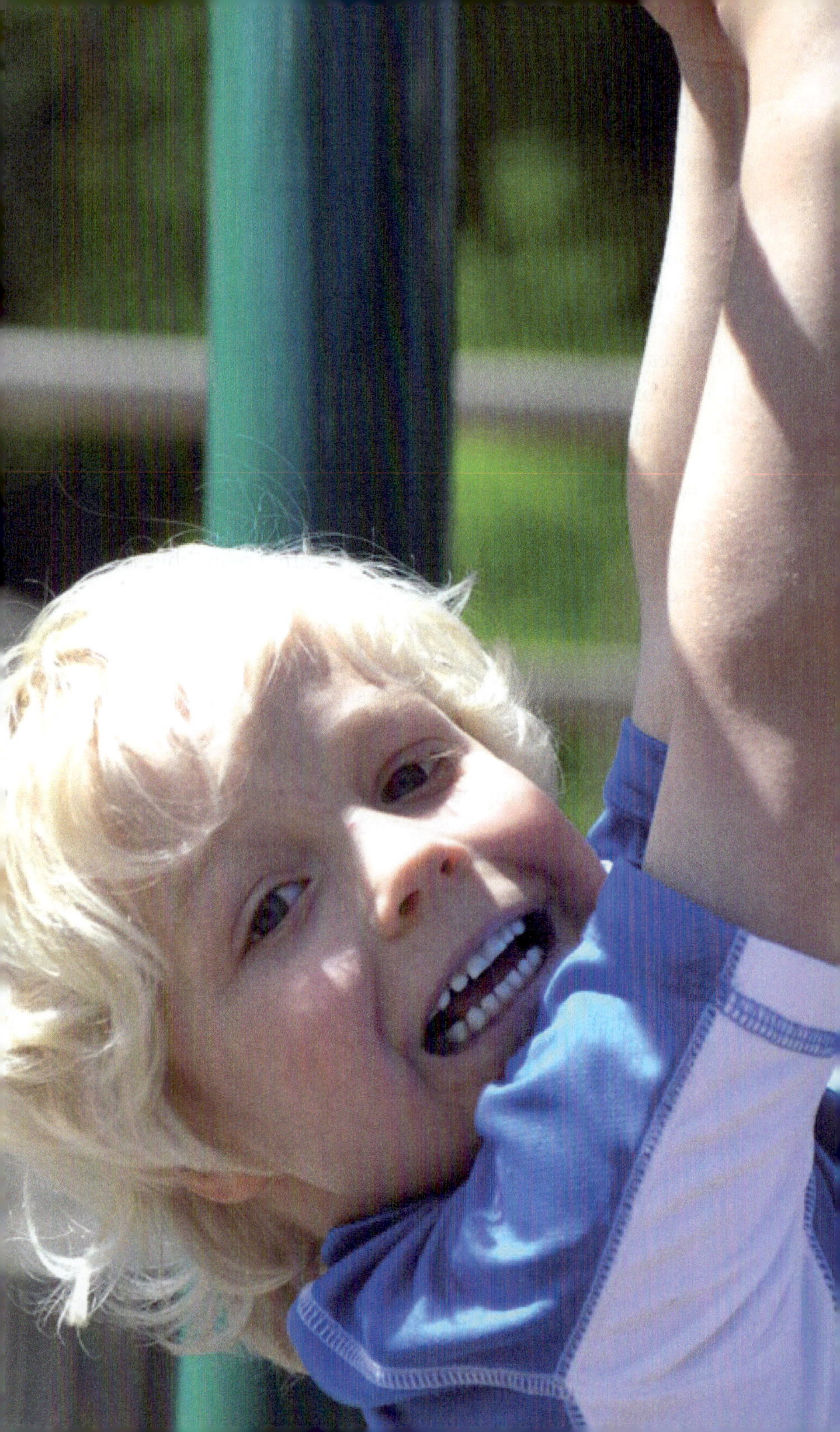

STRAWBERRY SHORTCAKE

1 slice Angel Food cake (1/12 of cake)
½ cup strawberries
Nonfat whipped topping

Place slice of angel food cake in small serving dish. Top with strawberries and a dollup of whipped topping.

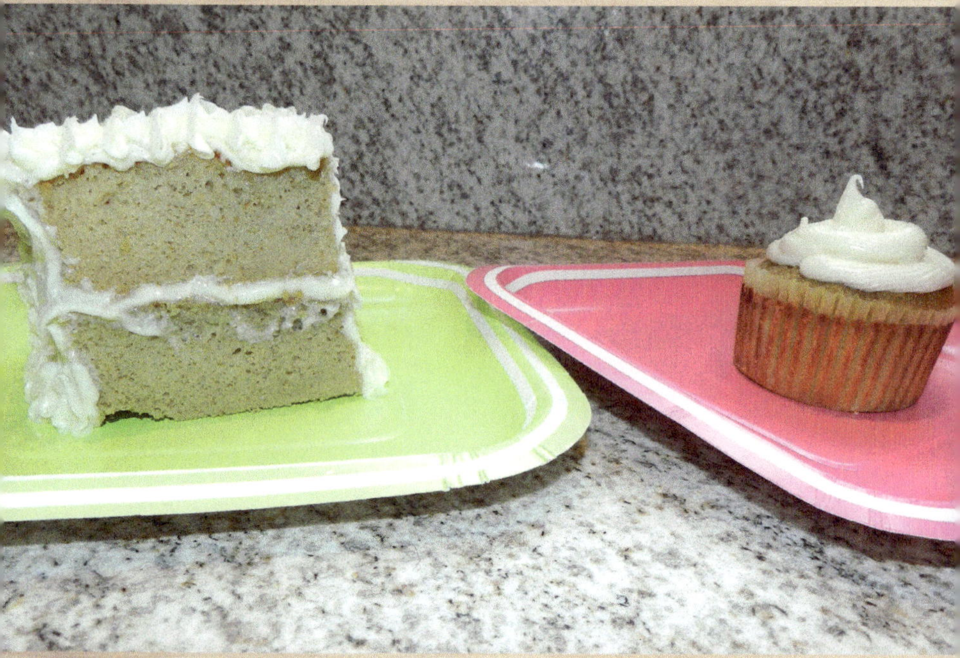

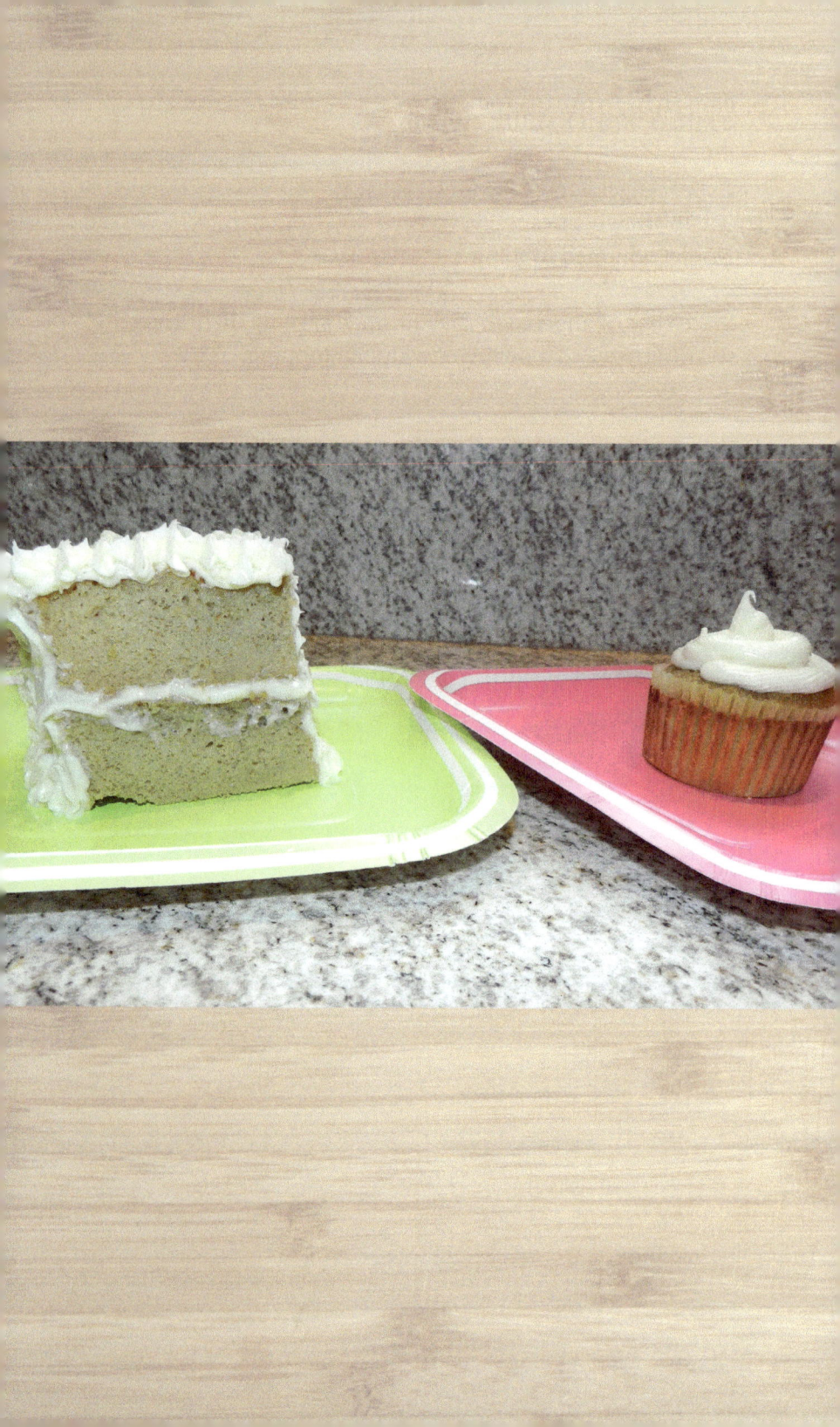

YELLOW CAKE
(also used for cupcakes)

Pillsbury sugar free yellow cake mix OR the following recipe adapted from www.healthyindulgences.net . So easy. So moist. NO, is does not taste like beans!!
**Makes single layer 9x9 cake or 12 cupcakes
** Make 24 hours ahead

1-15 oz can white beans, rinsed
5 large eggs plus 1 tsp coconut oil (or 1 egg yolk)
6 tablespoons unsalted butter
3/4 teaspoon pure Stevia extract
1/3 cup agave nectar (or honey)
4 teaspoons vanilla extract
6 packed tablespoons coconut flour (I have used whole wheat flour when in a bind and it worked fine)
1/2 teaspoon salt
1/2 teaspoon baking soda
1 teaspoon baking powder

- Preheat oven to 350 degrees.
- Put rinsed beans, eggs, oil (if using), vanilla, and salt in a food processor/blender and puree.
- In a large mixing bowl, cream softened butter and sweetener until smooth. Beat in pureed mixture.
- Add flour and the rest of the dry ingredients to the batter. Mix until blended well.
- If using as cake, prep pan: grease or spray pan, dust with flour covering bottom of pan discarding excess.
- If serving out of cake pan, place pan on wax paper and trace around with a toothpick. Cut out pan shape and line bottom of pan OR if making cupcakes, spray cupcake liners with cooking spray and spoon batter into cupcake liners until ¾ way full.
- Bake for 25 minutes for cupcakes. Bake 30-35 for cake.

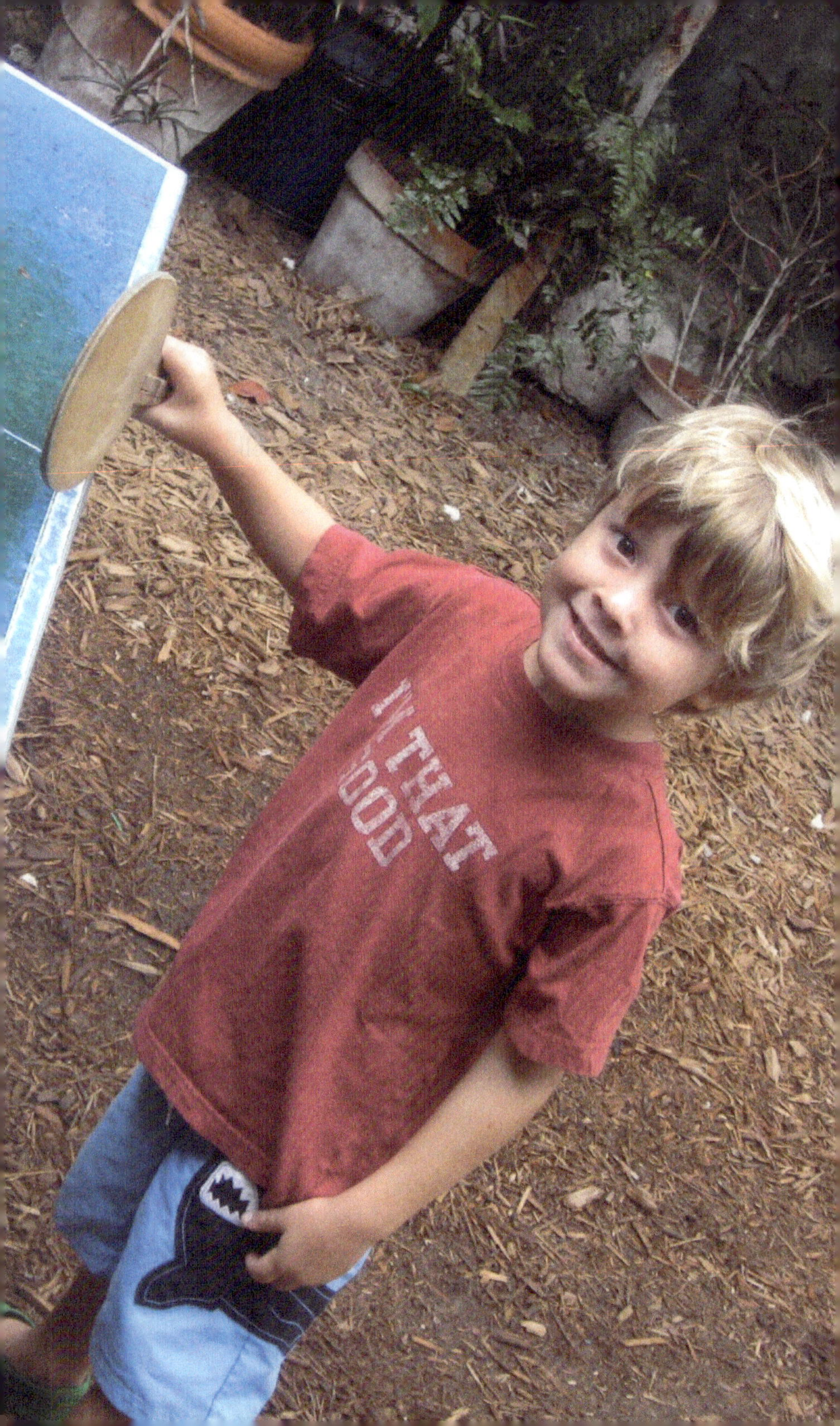
THAT

If serving cake on cake platter, once cooled, flip cake onto cake platter, cover and allow to sit 24 hours.

NOTE: *Allow to sit for 24 hours to eliminate "beany" taste.*

Vanilla frosting:
1 cup unsalted butter
¼ tsp salt
2 cups powdered sugar (see recipe this section. If not using recipe, then sift)
¼ cup skim milk
1 tsp vanilla

- Cream butter and salt in mixer.
- Gradually add sugar.
- Gradually add milk and vanilla.
- Mix until icing forms.

ABOUT THE AUTHOR

Thank you for buying my book. My name is Ashley Buescher. I am the mother of three girls ages 10, 14, and infant. In addition, I have been a nurse practitioner since January 1999. I created Kickin' It Kids for two reasons.

The first reason stems from my profession. I work with children ages 3-18. On a daily basis, I identify children who are at risk for becoming overweight, are overweight, or are obese. Unfortunately, I also diagnose these children with life-threatening health conditions such as high cholesterol, high blood pressure, or diabetes. In the 2011-2012 school year, my company referred over 30% of the children we saw for the above conditions. That statistic exceeds the alarming national statistic of children falling into the trend of obesity.

The second reason is personal. A health condition directly related to eating habits hit my household January 2012. I had to make drastic changes and make them quickly. You will read about my family's transformation in this book, *Your Kid's Favorite Meals Made Healthy! from shells'n'cheese to brownies, you will feel good about feeding your family!* My book offers close to 200 healthy recipes and snack ideas! Plus you will gain all the basic tools you need to transform any meal.

I learned quickly in my family's process that the transformation was going to go much smoother with peer support. This meant having friends over who enjoyed being active. Whether this meant riding bikes or doing 30 minutes of Wii Dance Party, the kids were having fun exercising together. Of course, the only snack options I offered were healthy. My children felt reassured and good about sharing this lifestyle change with peers. By now we all know that choices children and adults make will be influenced by lifestyles of those around them. Society worries so much about kids influencing kids in making negative lifestyle choices. I feel like we need to encourage kids to influence one another to make positive lifestyle choices. There is no greater "high" than eating right and exercising!!!

CPSIA information can be obtained at www.ICGtesting.com
Printed in the USA
LVOW011915100113

315163LV00006B/9/P